James Dunbar

Essays on the History of Mankind in Rude and Cultivated Ages

James Dunbar

Essays on the History of Mankind in Rude and Cultivated Ages

ISBN/EAN: 9783337311681

Printed in Europe, USA, Canada, Australia, Japan

Cover: Foto ©ninafisch / pixelio.de

More available books at **www.hansebooks.com**

ESSAYS

ON THE

HISTORY OF MANKIND

IN

RUDE AND CULTIVATED AGES.

By JAMES DUNBAR, LL. D.

PROFESSOR OF PHILOSOPHY IN THE KING'S COLLEGE
AND UNIVERSITY OF ABERDEEN.

LONDON:

PRINTED FOR W. STRAHAN; T. CADELL IN THE
STRAND; AND J. BALFOUR, EDINBURGH.
MDCCLXXX.

PREFACE.

TO folve fome appearances in civil life, and, by an appeal to the annals of mankind, to vindicate the character of the fpecies from vulgar prejudices, and thofe of philofophic theory, is the aim of the Volume now delivered to the Public. Its contents are digefted on a regular plan; though the loofer form of Effays has been preferred to a more fyftematic arrangement.

He who attempts to reform the world is actuated by a wild enthufiafm, or by a divine impulfe. To ftop the career of Vice, is the ultimate end of well-directed ambition. That

ambition

ambition was felt by the great writers of antiquity. They erected a temple to Virtue, and exhausted on the opposite character all the thunder of eloquence.

Animated with the views, not with the genius of the ancients, I occupy the same ground; for on that ground the efforts of inferior men may be of use.

Every Author is a candidate for the public favour, and the Public alone is the arbiter of his fate. With such a sanction he will not need, and without it he ought to decline, even the patronage of kings.

The voice of the Public, like the voice of an oracle, it becomes an Author to hear with respectful silence.

Even

Even while it mortifies, it inftructs; while it refufes approbation, it teaches wifdom. It checks ambition in its wild career; and reminds the candidate for fame to return into that *deceiving path* of *life**, from which he ought not to have deviated, and which, how mortifying foever to the Author, is perhaps the happieft for the Man.

* Fallentis femita vitæ.

CONTENTS.

CONTENTS.

CONTENTS.

ERRATA.

Page 48, line 5. For *natural the*, read *the natural.*
Page 150, line 16. For *exhibited*, read *expected.*
Page 151, line 21. For *work*, read *waste.*

ESSAYS

ON THE

HISTORY OF MANKIND.

ESSAYS

ON THE

HISTORY OF MANKIND.

ESSAY I.

ON THE PRIMEVAL FORM OF SOCIETY.

HUMAN Nature, in fome refpects, is fo various and fluctuating; fo altered, or fo difguifed by external things, that its independent character has become dark and problematical. The hiftory of its exertions in their primeval form, would reflect a light upon moral and political fcience, which we endeavour in vain to

B   collect

collect in the annals of polished nations. What pity is it, that, the transactions of this early period being consigned to eternal oblivion, history is necessarily defective in opening the scene of man!

Consistently, however, with present appearances, and with the memorials of antiquity, the following changes, it is pretended, may have arisen successively to the species.

First, Man may have subsisted, in some sort, like other animals, in a separate and individual state, before the date of language, or the commencement of any regular intercourse.

Secondly, He may be contemplated in a higher stage; a proficient in language, and a member of that artless community which consists with equality, with freedom, and independence.

Last

Laſt of all, by ſlow and imperceptible tranſitions, he ſubſiſts and flouriſhes under the protection and diſcipline of civil government. It is the deſign of this Eſſay to enquire into the principles which either ſuperſeded the firſt, or haſtened the ſecond ſtate; and led to an harmonious and ſocial correſpondence, antecedently to the æra of ſubordination, to the grand enterpriſes of art, to the inſtitution of laws, or any of the arrangements of nations. But it is the order of improvement merely, not the chronological order of the world, that belongs to this enquiry. Degeneracy, as well as improvement, is incident to man: and we are not here concerned with the original perfection of his nature, nor with the circumſtances wherein he was placed at the beginning by his Creator.

There is one general obſervation ſtrongly applicable, in all ages, to human nature: the appearance of proper objects is eſſential

to

to the exertion of its powers. As therefore there are talents belonging to individuals, which, for want of their objects,
have lain for ever dormant; so perhaps there
are talents inherent in the species which at
no time have been called forth into action,
and which may yet appear conspicuous in
some succeeding period. Any alteration
in the human fabric would seem to affect
the identity of our being; but from the
novelty and variety of the objects with
which it is conversant, the Soul of man
may become progressive; and without un-
dergoing any actual transformation in its
powers, may open and expand itself in
energy through the successive periods of
duration. The celebrated * distinctions of
Aristotle will then appear to have an ample
foundation in nature. Thus much is certain, a mutual intercourse gradually opens
latent powers; and the extension of this
intercourse is generally attended with new

* Ἐντελεχεια and Δυναμις.

exertions

exertions of intellect. Withdraw this intercourse, and what is man! " Let all the powers and elements of nature (fays an illuftrious philofopher) confpire to ferve and obey one man : let the fun rife and fet at his command : the fea and rivers roll as he pleafes, and the earth furnifh fpontaneoufly whatever may be ufeful or agreeable to him : he will ftill be miferable till you give him fome one perfon at leaft, with whom he may fhare his happinefs, and whofe efteem and friendfhip he may enjoy."

Society then is the theatre on which our genius expands with freedom. It is effential to the origin of all our ideas of natural and of moral beauty. It is the prime mover of all our inventive powers. Every effort, beyond what is merely animal, has a reference to a community; and the folitary favage, who traverfes the defert, is fcarce raifed fo far by nature above other animals,

as

as he is funk by fortune beneath the ftandard of his own race.

The deftitute condition of man, as an animal, has been an ufual topic of declamation among the learned; and this alone, according to fome theories, is the foundation both of focial union and of civil combinations.

After the population of the world, and the growth of arts, mutual alliances and mutual fupport became indeed effential in our divided fyftem : and it is no wonder if certain appearances in the civil æra have been transferred, in imagination, to all preceding times. At firft, however, it may be queftioned, whether there reigned not fuch an independence in our œconomy, as is obfervable in other parts of the creation.

It is the arts of life which, by enervating our corporeal powers, and multiplying the objects of defire, have annihilated per-

fonal

fonal independence, and formed an immenfe chain of connexions among collective bodies. Nor is it perhaps fo much
the call of neceffity, or mutual wants, as
a certain delight in their kind congenial
with all natures, which conftitutes the
fundamental principle of affociation and
harmony throughout the whole circle of
being. But man, it is pretended, by
nature timid, runs to *fociety* for relief; and
finds an afylum there. Nor is he fingular
in this: all animals in the hour of danger
crowd together, and derive confidence and
fecurity from mutual aid.

Danger, however, it may be anfwered, far
from fuggefting a confederacy, tends in moft
cafes to diffolve rather than to confirm the
union. Secure from danger, animals herd
together, and feem to difcover a compla-
cency towards their kind. Let but a fingle
animal of more rapacious form prefent
himfelf to view, they inftantly difperfe;

they

they derive no fecurity from mutual aid, and rarely attempt to fupply their weaknefs in detail, by their collective ftrength. This fingle animal is a match for thoufands of a milder race. The law of dominion in the fcale of life is the ftrength of the individual merely, not the number of the tribe; and of all animals, man almoft alone becomes confiderable by the combination of his fpecies.

In fociety, animals are rather more prone to timidity from the prevalence of the fofter inftincts. Thofe of the ravenous clafs, generally the moft folitary, are accordingly the moft courageous; and man himfelf declines in courage in proportion to the extent of his alliances: not indeed in that fpecies of it which is the genuine offspring of magnanimity and heroic fentiment; but in that conftitutional boldnefs and temerity which refides, if I may fay fo, in our animal nature. Hence intrepidity is a predominant
nant

nant feature in the favage character: hence the favage himfelf, feparately bold and undaunted, when he acts in concert with his fellows is found liable to panic from this public fympathy, this reciprocal collifion of minds. And it is hence, perhaps, according to the obfervation of a diftinguifh-ed writer [*A*], that the moft fignal victories recorded in the annals of nations have been uniformly obtained by the army of inferior number.

But to return to the analogy of animals: I am not ignorant that fome are gregarious from neceffity, are formed for offenfive or defenfive wars, and require joint labour for their fubfiftence or accommodation. Yet in fuch examples the common functions are directed by inftinct rather than by art; and evidence lefs the policy of the animal, than, if I may call it fo, the policy of nature. When thefe provinces [*B*] are well defined, many

of

of the appearances we fo much admire
will no longer be regarded as marks of
invention, or concerted plan. Where
there is no option, there is no agency;
and within a contracted fphere, while
feparate acts of fagacity in various tribes
are fo often obfervable, their concurring
efforts are comparatively rare. Each
creature below us is conftituted the fole
guardian of its own privileges, feems,
as it were, a feparate fyftem, and the refources of its own conftitution its natural
and its only fupport. Even the union
of the fexes, formed for the continuance
of the kind, is a temporary union, and
diffolves at the inftant when its operations
are no longer neceffary. As for larger
conventions, they are often purely cafual;
and the invitation of the fame pafture will
at times folve fuch appearances, without
reforting to the ties either of dependence
or of love. It is thus the fowls of the air
alight fo often on the fame field. Thus the
ravens

ravens and other creatures of prey convene around the body of a dead animal. And thus the infect tribes are wont to affemble on the fame putrefaction in fuch amazing fwarms, that naturalifts have been feduced, by the appearance, into the belief of an equivocal generation, as if thefe infects were actually produced from the mafs of corruption on which they feed.

An opinion of intercourfe in the lower ranks of being is often fuggefted or favoured by a propenfity there is in man, to confer on every creature a portion of his own nature. Suitable to this propenfity, in obferving a concourfe of animals, however fortuitous, he magnifies every appearance in favour of the focial principle, and prefumes a concert and government where none in reality fubfift. It is the fame propenfity which gives life to inanimate objects, and leads us fo irrefiftibly, on fome occafions, to confider them as active and percipient

cipient beings. Withdraw the aid of imagination, and the embellifhments of fiction,
and much of that intercourfe is deftroyed,
which we prefume to reign in many departments of the animal world.

Yet if urgent neceffity did not produce
a feparation, it is probable that the love of
herding would be univerfal. Animals, accordingly, that are folitary in one country,
are gregarious in another. Even the antipathies among different tribes neceffity
often creates. For in fome regions of the
globe, where that neceffity does not fubfift,
animals of prey fufpend their hoftilities;
and tribes, ufually accounted the moft im-
placable by nature, fulfil, in harmony,
their peculiar deftinations, without en-
croaching on each other's happinefs or
fecurity [C].

Upon the whole, we may pronounce
that interefted intercourfe in the animal

kingdom,

kingdom, is greater in appearance than in reality; that the concourfe of a tribe is often accidental; that all regular œconomy is under the direction of inftinct; and that in all the freer combinations, the fociety is held together by the tie of affection or confcious delight, more than by fear, or mutual wants, or any neceffary call of nature.

Such is the conftitution of the inferior creation. Is the fame analogy obferved in man? Was he ever in this independent and individual ftate? Or wherein does his pre-eminence confift? Not, furely, in the mechanifm of thofe inftincts which direct him to procure fubfiftence. The fenfes of other animals are as acute as his. Not in achievements by bodily ftrength. For, in that particular, many of them far fur-pafs him. Not in performing *jointly*, what fo many other creatures can perform apart.

Mani-

Manifeftly, that would be no perfection.
But in this his pre-eminence confifts, that
being as independent as they in all the corporeal functions, impelled by no neceffity,
but by generous paffions, he rifes to improvements which flow from the union of
his kind.

In fome parts of our conftitution, it
cannot be denied, we refemble the other
animals. If therefore a time was when
thofe parts chiefly or alone were exercifed, our objects, and purfuits, and habits
of living muft have been nearly fimilar. I am far from affirming that ever
there was no diftinction. At all times, in
our walk, there is fome nobler aim. There
is fome inward confcioufnefs, fome decifive
mark of fuperiority in every condition of
men. But the line which meafures that
fuperiority is of very variable extent.
Let us allow but equal advantages from

culture

culture to the mind and body; and it is consequential to infer, that savages, in some of the wilder forms, must be as inferior to civilized man in intellectual abilities, and in the peculiar graces of the mind, as they surpass him in the activity of their limbs, in the command of their bodies, and in the exertion of all the meaner functions. Some striking instances of savage tribes with so limited an understanding, as is scarce capable of forming any arrangement for futurity, are produced by an Historian who traces the progress of human reason through various stages of improvement, and unites truth with eloquence in his descriptions of mankind *.

In some corners of the globe, if we may credit report, man and beast lead in the forest a sort of promiscuous life; and the boundary is scarce discernible which divides

* History of America, v. i. p. 309.

the

the rational from the animal world. This fact, no doubt magnified by travellers and historians, and tortured in the theories of philosophy, has however some foundation, and is in part consonant to our own experience. The progress of nations and of men, though not exactly parallel, is found in several respects to correspond: and in the interval from infancy to manhood, we may remark this gradual opening of the human faculties. First of all, those of sense appear, grow up spontaneously, or require but little culture. Next in order, the propensities of the heart display their force; a fellow-feeling with others unfolds itself gradually on the appearance of proper objects; for man becomes sociable long before he is a rational being. Last in the train, the powers of intellect begin to blossom, are reared up by culture, and demand an intercourse of minds.

When

When we obferve, then, this analogy between the individual and the fpecies; when we obferve the gradation of improvement, and the flow departure of man from the confines of animal life; is there no intimation here concerning his original ftate, or rather concerning that ftate which human nature uninformed, and unenlightened by providence, muft have at firft affumed? When arts and dependence grow together, and fubfift fo nearly in the fame proportion, ought we not to regard them in the relation of caufe and effect, and confequently allow of little or no dependence before the birth of arts? But the arts are formed in the bofom of fociety. Society therefore had another origin than mutual dependence and mutual wants. It is not, if I may fay fo, the fickly daughter of calamity, nor even the production of an afpiring underftanding, but the free and legitimate offspring of the human heart.

C   Yet

Yet the attempt were vain to refer the origin of large communities to domestic relation and the ties of blood.

That *natural affection* * which belongs to man belongs also to the inferior classes, and subsists among them with equal vigour. In both, the mechanism is the same, and calculated with the same design. At first therefore, perhaps, it was proportioned to the exigency of things, and as in them, so in us likewise, of limited duration. The period of *gestation*, in animals, is so contrived as to prevent all possibility of incumbrance from a second brood. But the period of *pregnancy*, it is allowed, were by far too short to dispense, in the human species, with the parental cares. The connexion, therefore, is necessarily more durable, its functions more various and progressive, and suited to the different ages and circumstances of a connected and rising progeny. Yet the im-

* Στοργη.

provements

provements of focial life, by the introduction of order, and by refining on all
the paffions and feelings of our frame,
have given to this inftinct a perpetuity unknown in the primeval ftate.

Prior to fingle marriages, and the more
accurate afcertainment of families, an uncertainty with regard to the progeny muft
have often fuppreffed the inftinct in the
breaft of the one parent; and in the breaft
of the other parent, the equal licence of both
tended ultimately to its extinction or decay.
It is obfervable, even in our own times,
that the affections of a woman, mother to
feveral diftinct families, are exceedingly
liable to be eftranged from the children of
a former bed [D]. This remark on the
female character is at leaft as ancient as
Homer.

Even Ulyffes's queen was not prefumed
exempt from a frailty fo natural to her

fex.

fex. The young prince of Ithaca is accordingly warned by Minerva to return home, before abfence and new engagements had eftranged the heart of Penelope from the fon of Ulyffes.

> " Thou know'ft the practice of the female train.
> " Loft in the children of the prefent fpoufe,
> " They flight the pledges of their former vows;
> " Their love is always with the lover paft,
> " Still the fucceeding flame expels the laft."
>
> Odyffey, B. xv. v. 24.

Is love then at firft devoted to a fingle object? Is fuch abfolute confinement of appetite a maxim of uninftructed nature? The fuppofition, though it were not repugnant to every mode of appetite, and to the wilder range of life, is irreconcileable with the hiftory of the ruder ages. Some latitude, in this refpect, is almoft univerfal after fociety has received a form; and by

5   degrees

degrees only is eſtabliſhed that ſtricter rule which is ſo often violated, when connected with the moral harmony of the world, and guarded by the ſanctions of divine and human laws [E]. The intereſt of a family, the order of ſociety, juſtifies the reſtraint. Even the amorous paſſion, when aſſociated with moral ſentiment, leads to an excluſive and indiſſoluble union; and the ſweets of domeſtic life make ample amends for its moſt ſevere engagements. But this adjuſtment of things ſeems to be an improvement, or refinement on the firſt œconomy; owing its original either directly to divine command, or to the wiſdom of human policy.

In ſome rude countries, according to the information of modern travellers, rendered credible by ſeveral paſſages of antiquity, the women are not only at the head of domeſtic government, but poſſeſs a voice

C 3 and

and afcendency in public councils and deliberations [F].

Here then is probably difplayed a peculiar and ftriking effect of gratitude and
natural authority; and the weaker fex,
though deftined in the intermediate ages
of barbarifm to the moft deplorable fubjection, have derived from the love and
reverence of children, who know no other
parent, a rank and confideration fuperior
to what the rules of gallantry or generofity prefcribe among the moft refined
nations.

On the commencement of domeftic order,
filial reverence, one of the ftrongeft fentiments that can touch the heart, fails not
to recognize its object, and acts with re-
doubled vigour when accumulated in one
direction. A variety of circumftances
augments its force; and that natural love
which

which feems not, in any other fpecies, to afcend from the young to the parent, afcends in ours with the firft dawnings of reafon and morality, and forms a diftin- guifhing characteriftic of human kind.   •

But as, in fuch inftances, the *paternal* inftincts are of more precarious exertion, at an æra further back, the *maternal* in- ftincts likewife may have been conftituted in circumftances which render them fluctu- ating and temporary.

It is not then fuch partial principles which could have formed or embodied the larger communities of mankind. It is not a parent, a child, or a brother, but the fpecies itfelf, that is the object em- braced by humanity. In fome cafes, per- ᾽ haps, the patriarchal government may have furnifhed the model of a larger plan ; but mankind were before in poffeffion of the fweets of an independent fociety. The mem-

bers

bers of a family became members of this fociety, before they became members of a ftate.
A thoufand circumftances in the range of
being, convening numbers of the fpecies on
the fame ftage, muft have prefented the op-
portunities of focial life. The only queftion
is, how regular intercourfe was formed,
how ftrangers were converted into acquaintance, and how thofe who came together
at firft by accident came afterwards to
affemble by appointment.

With fimilar appetites and congenial
paffions, the excurfions of individuals will
often coincide. They will be found occafionally on the banks of the fame river, or
in the fame corner of the grove. The
reiterated appearance of the objects flowly
and imperceptibly calls forth new defires.
Each interview has its effect. The brutality of the favage begins to vanifh. Some
refinement appears. An appetite for fociety ripens, which afterwards muft be
gratified

gratified as well as other appetites. Little plans are carried on in concert; and at a time when no difcordant interefts, or various purfuits, had diverfified the fcene, a fmall community might be kept together by the tie of fociability and reciprocal love.

In thefe days of envy, and of intereft, we are little able to conceive its force; nor, if the feelings remained, could artificial language, in this refpect, fupply the language of nature. When fimilar functions and occupations in civil fociety prove fo often a bond of union among thofe of the fame order, how immenfe muft have been the effect of an exact conformity of life! That refemblance of difpofition and of character, which is the cement of little affociations, and is the principle of private friendfhip, was the original bafis of public union. The hiftory of the Soldurii in Gaul, of the ancient Germans, and of other public bodies, whereof there are fo many

examples

examples in the fimple ages, evidences the
ftability of thofe facred bonds and confederacies that originate in the heart. The
hiftory too of fome of the South Sea ifles,
which the late voyages of difcovery have
tended to difclofe, enables us to glance at
fociety in fome of its earlier forms, and to
mark, in fome ftriking examples, the in-
violable fidelity of focial love.

The principles of union are, in the
order of things, prior to the principles of
hoftility. The former are, in truth, productive of the latter, which, in a more
advanced period, burfting forth, like a torrent, againft other tribes, disfigures the
character of uncivilized nations.

The affections of the heart are of limited
exertion; and that mutual love, which is
confined within a narrow fphere, triumphs,
as it were, over the fentiment which gave

it

it birth, and creates, in a competition of interests, such fierce animosity among contending tribes.

As emigrants in rude ages usually pass their own frontiers with hostile minds, they are regarded by others with a jealous eye; and in the penury of language, a *stranger* and an *enemy* may receive one common name. It was thus the ancient Romans, addicted to piracy and war, and consequently jealous of the designs of others, used the same term in both these senses; for this is more probable far, according to the observation of an ingenious modern, than the solution of *Tully*, who takes occasion, from this coincidence, to extol the humanity of his ancestors. But such criticisms affect not the general history of rude nations. When there is no ground of variance, the original sentiment revives in all its force, the rights of

hospitality

hofpitality are peculiarly revered, and an unfufpected ftranger is embraced with a fondnefs and cordiality which redeems the character of the fpecies.

Thus have we reached that univerfal principle which reigns, in fome degree, in every diftrict of nature. The moft rapacious of animals confefs its power; and, while at war with the reft of the creation, fympathize with each other, and refufe to tafte the blood of any of their own kind. This harmony of things, fo confpicuous in the inferior orders of life, feems to affront the conduct of the rational fpecies. Moralifts and poets have availed themfelves of this topic, and inveigh with indignant fpirit againft that proftitution of fentiment, which, forming an exception to a law almoft univerfal, requires the effufion of human blood. Thus the Roman poet ex-

poftulates

postulates with a degenerate age in these admirable lines:

> ———Quando leoni
> Fortior eripuit vitam leo? quo nemore
>   unquam
> Expiravit aper majoris dentibus apri?
> Indica tigris agit rabida cum tigride pacem
> Perpetuam: fævis inter se convenit ursis.
> Aft homini———
>
> Juv. Sat. xv. lib. 5.

Such reproaches indeed are chargeable on mankind; but touch not the clear dictates of morality, nor the primeval rectitude of the heart.

The great lines of humanity are legible in all communities; and it is the description of every country under heaven,

> ———Sunt hic etiam sua præmia laudi;
> Sunt lachrymæ rerum, et mentem mortalia
>   tangunt.

The love of the species is the grand principle of attraction, as essential to the
rational,

rational, and, in some degree, to the animal, as gravitation to the material world:
nor wilder were the attempt to expound
the harmony of the solar system from the
limited attraction of magnetism, than to
expound the combination of tribes, and the
moral harmony of nations, from the operation of partial instincts. Even pride, the
passion which divides mankind, was originally a principle of union. It was a sense
of the dignity of the species, not an
opinion of superiority among individuals;
and with exalted notions of their own
rank, they reserved for the inferior creatures that sovereign contempt which they
can now bestow so liberally on their fellow
men.

In such circumstances it was impossible
for mankind not to meditate, from the
beginning, a separation from the life of
brutes. They must have conceived the
plan of holding the dominion of the world;
and

and actuated with a decent pride, the confcioufnefs of their own pre-eminence, they
became daily more and more fufceptible of
reafon, of morality, and of religion. Thus
are the foundations laid, upon which were
afterwards reared, by flow advances, the
fuperftructure of policy and arts. In fociety
the faculties have an object. The fprings
of ingenuity are put into motion; and the
language of nature gradually participates
of art. The efforts of genius excite admiration. The acquifitions of induftry, or
invention, confer a right which fuggefts
the idea of property; and the diftinctions
of natural talents lay a foundation for
correfponding diftinctions in fociety.

But thefe inventions and improvements,
which do honour to our nature, tended at
the fame time to divide mankind. On this
account it may be queftioned, whether the
enlargement of our faculties, and all the

6   advan-

advantages from arts, counterbalance the feuds and animofities which they foon introduced into the world. The ferene and joyous interval between the rudenefs of mere animal life, and the diffenfions of civil fociety, conftituted, perhaps, that fhort but happy period, to which antiquity refers in her defcriptions of the golden age.

No theory, indeed, in morals, or in go-vernment, was then devifed. Yet moral rules were feldom broken, when an equal and generous commerce was the rule of government. And it is amufing to obferve into what abfurdities fpeculative men have been fo often carried upon thefe fubjects by prefumption, by affectation, or by the love of paradox.

Hence a variety of theories, ancient and modern, concerning the origin of moral fentiment.

Epicurus

Epicurus obferving the external advantages refulting to the individual from moral conduct, purfued the idea fo far as to allow fuperior advantages, and pleafures of a higher relifh, altogether to efcape his notice. It is indeed ftrange that any obferver fhould omit this obvious comment on human life, That to be the object of love, of efteem, and of refpect, is in itfelf far more defirable than all the confequences with regard to external eafe and fecurity that can be derived from that fountain. But Epicurus could contemplate beauty neither in nature nor in man. And what better could be expected from the philofopher who had afcribed the origin of worlds to a fortuitous concourfe of atoms ?

A Writer of the laft age, in the compofition of a philofophical romance, is ftill more extravagant.

D   All

All virtue, according to him, confifts in obedience to the public magiftrate; and all moral obligations are the offspring of civil government.

But has government, it may be afked, any creative power? Or whence the duty of allegiance, if there was no primeval law? Would not Amphion and Orpheus have ftrung their lyres in vain?

It is no wonder that the fame writer fhould arraign the genius of the ancient republics, and condemn to the flames all Greek and Roman learning as a fovereign expedient for ftrengthening the hands of government.

But I am not called upon, by my fub-ject, to explain or to refute fuch fyftems. And I fhall content myfelf with obferving, that a late publication, much read and admired in our fafhionable world, is more

8   danger-

dangerous than any speculative theory to the morals of the rising generation. As patrons of licentiousness, Epicurus and Hobbes, and even Machiavel and Mandeville, must bow to the noble author.

It is in the spirit of his performance to separate the *honestum* from the *decorum* of life; to insult whatever is venerable in domestic alliance; to substitute artificial manners in the room of the natural; to raise superficial above solid accomplishment, and to hold up dissimulation and imposture as the essentials of character.

This is a species of refinement avowed in no former age. It contains a solecism in education, and in the œconomy of civil affairs.

To exalt the *Graces* above Virtue, is, if I may say so, to exalt creatures above their Creator. The *Graces* are chiefly amiable as emblems of Virtue. Break this alliance, and they are no more. Unite them with the oppofite character, and this fantaftical con-junction renders a monfter ftill more deformed. For my own part, I had as foon behold the monfter itfelf in all the horrors of its native deformity, as in fuch infolent attire.

The *Graces* are the handmaids of Virtue, not the fovereigns; and all their honours are derived. But Virtue, though naked and unadorned, were Virtue ftill.

Quam ardentes amores non excitaret fui,
 fi videretur !

How different was the conduct of a Ro-man ftatefman, when, in the perfon of a father, he delivered inftructions to youth ! The inftructions of the Roman fill the young with rapture. Thofe of the Briton excite indignation in the aged. But I afk pardon of the reader, when I name the Britifh author in the fame breath with Cicero.

Cicero. And if the fyftem of the noble lord was defigned merely for the courtier, with the courtier let it reft. Without the formality of fyftem, the ftrict obfervance of moral rules is difpenfed with in the negociations of courts.

Let it be numbered then among courtly privileges to patronize deceit. When perfidy and diffimulation are declared by patent to belong to the members of the diplomatic body, they will become, perhaps, more emphatically, the reprefentatives of kings.

But while things are thus adjufted to the meridian of courts; while the *civil code*, in many countries, is no more than the breath of kings; and, in all countries, may be diffolved by legiflative power; the *moral code*, which is paramount to all civil authority; and from which all civil obligations arife, remains eternally in force.

It

It was delivered from heaven to the people, and to maintain its authority is the *jus divinum* of nations.

With thefe fentiments I clofe the Effay: and fuch fentiments are addreffed more particularly to the Britifh youth by one of their public guardians, who then only feels the full importance of his ftation when he animates the rifing generation in the purfuits of honour.

N O T E S.

NOTE [*A*], p. 9.

SIR William Temple, in an Essay on Heroic Virtue, defcends into the following detail, which, on account of its importance, I lay before my Readers, in the words of that intelligent and agreeable Writer.

" The fecond obfervation I fhall make upon
" the fubject of victory and conquest is, that
" they have in general been made by the fmaller
" numbers over the greater; againft which I
" do not remember any exception in all the
" famous battles regiftered in ftory, excepting
" that of Tamerlane and Bajazet, whereof the
" firft is faid· to have exceeded about a fourth
" part in number, though they were fo vaft on
" both fides that they were not very eafy to be
" well accounted. For the reft, the numbers
" of the Perfians with Cyrus were fmall to
" thofe of the Affyrians: thofe of the Mace-
" donians

" donians were in no battle againſt the Perſians
" above forty thouſand men, though ſome-
" times againſt three, four, or ſix hundred
" thouſand.

" The Athenian army little exceeded ten
" thouſand, and fighting for the liberties of
" their country, beat above ſix ſcore thouſand
" Perſians at Marathon.

" The Lacedemonians, in all the famous
" exploits of that ſtate, never had above twelve
" thouſand Spartans in the field at a time, and
" ſeldom above twenty thouſand men with their
" allies.

" The Romans ever fought with ſmaller
" againſt greater numbers, unleſs in the battles
" of Cannæ and Thraſymene, which were the
" only famous ones they loſt againſt foreign
" enemies; and Cæſar's army at Pharſalia, as
" well as in Gaul and Germany, were in no
" proportion to thoſe he conquered. That of
" Marius was not above forty thouſand againſt
" three hundred thouſand Cimbers. The famous
" victories of Ætius and Beliſarius againſt the
" barbarous northern nations were with mighty
" diſproportion of numbers, as likewiſe the firſt
                              " victories

" victories of the Turks upon the Perfian king-
" dom; of the Tartars upon the Chinefe: and
" Scanderbeg never faw together above fixteen
" thoufand men in all the renowned victories
" he achieved againft the Turks, though in
" number fometimes above a hundred thou-
" fand.

" To defcend to later times, the Englifh
" victories fo renowned at Creffy, and Poictiers,
" and Agincourt, were gained with difadvan-
" tages of numbers out of all proportion. The
" great achievements of Charles VIII. in Italy,
" of Henry IV. in France, and of Guftavus
" Adolphus in Germany, were ever performed
" with 'fmaller againft greater numbers; and
" among all the exploits which have fo juftly
" raifed the reputation and honour of Monf.
" Turenne for the greateft Captain in his time,
" I do not remember any of them were achieved
" without difadvantage of number; and the
" late defeat of the Turks at the fiege of
" Vienna, which faved Chriftendom, and has
" eternized the memory of the duke of Lor-
" raine, was too frefh and great an example of
" this affertion to need any more, or leave it in
" difpute." Upon thefe inconteftible facts the
argument proceeds thus: " If it be true, which
" I think

" I think will not be denied, that the battle is
" loft where the fright firft enters, then the
" reafon will appear why victory has generally
" followed the fmaller numbers; becaufe, in a
" body compofed of more parts, it may fooner
" enter upon one than in that which confifts of
" fewer, as likelier to find ten wife men toge-
" ther than an hundred, and an hundred fear-
" lefs men than a thoufand. And thofe who
" have the fmaller forces endeavour moft to
" fupply that defect by the choice difcipline
" and bravery of their troops; and where the
" fright once enters an army, the greater the
" number the greater the diforder, and thereby
" the lofs of the battle more certain and
" fudden."

The truth of the above might be illuftrated
by more recent examples, and a more copious
induction. The obfervation, fince our Author's
time, is confirmed by the experience of another
century. In the memorable battle of Plaffy,
the Englifh army under Lord Clive defeated
an enemy which outnumbered them ten to one.

The King of Pruffia's battles in the laft war
would form a feries of fplendid examples in
fupport of the fame conclufion, if the fuperior
abilities

abilities of that great Prince were not alone fufficient to account for his fuperiority in arms.

But the facts above fpecified are fully fufficient for the afcertainment of fo curious a phænomenon, on the caufes of which our Author has defcanted with fo much ability.

Note [B], p. 9.

THERE are certain principles in the conftitution both of men and animals, which lead blindly and irrefiftibly to unknown ends. To thefe we give the name of *inftinct*; and to define its exertions in all their variety and extent, forms one of the nicest queftions in philofophy. The province of *reafon* having been confined to abftract conclufions, it has been doubted whether it belongs at all to animals; and habits and inftincts have been deemed fufficient to account for their whole œconomy. Jealous of our prerogative, we would not have inferior creatures to claim, in this particular, any kindred with the human mind.

It is however certain, that animals are capable of recollection, and of forefight; and by confequence poffefs the faculty which infers the future

future from the paſt. Many of them too diſcover an inventive faculty; and when drawn
into artificial circumſtances beyond their uſual
tract of life, extricate themſelves with an addreſs
and ſagacity that would be deemed rational in
man. Admitting then to animals ſome degree
of reaſon, as well as inſtinct, it is of importance
to define their reſpective functions.

It is one criterion of *inſtinct* to be uniform in
its proceedings : *reaſon* is various, and ſuppoſes
a choice. The one principle, as far as it extends, is infallible in its determinations; but
the other principle is liable to error. The one
acquires maturity at once, and ſuperſedes experience, and is incapable of culture. The other
is guided by experience, and ſtands in need of
culture, and arrives gradually at different ſtages
of perfection.

Inſtinct is fixed and immutable, not in the
fabric only of a ſingle animal; the ſame exertions of it are common to the ſpecies. But
reaſon, which becomes more or leſs perfect in
the ſame individual, is dealt out in various
meaſure and proportion to the ſeveral individuals of the kind.

Theſe.

Thefe principles feem counterparts to each other in the fyftem of creation. In proportion as the one is denied, the other comes in aid of the defect.

The perfection of reafon would fuperfede the neceffity of inftinct; but its imperfection calls aloud for this auxiliary.

Inftinct accordingly is, in the human fpecies, more confpicuous in infancy than in manhood; and reigns moft abfolutely in all the meaner departments of animal life. The fowls of the air, the fifhes of the fea, and the infect tribes, feem wifer, in this refpect, than *he* who ftyles himfelf Lord of the Creation.

But is this the wifdom of the animal? It is rather the wifdom of nature.

——Hinc ille avium concentus in agris,
Et lætæ pecudes, & ovantes gutture corvi.

Nature has drawn a veil over this part of her proceedings, and that veil what mortal can remove? At leaft fure I am, I may apply to my own fpeculations on this myfterious theme what the poet Simonides, when revolving on

the

the nature of the gods, obferved to the King of
Syracufe,

Quanto diutius confidero, tanto mihi res videtur
   obfcurior.

NOTE [*C*], p. 12.

A Navigator, whofe prefent voyage, we hope,
      for the honour of civilized nations, will
not be difturbed by the prefent hoftilities, thus
defcribes, in a former voyage, the condition of
animals on a fequeftered ifland, near Staten-
land in the South Sea.

" It is amazing to fee how the different ani-
" mals which inhabit this little fpot are mutually
" reconciled. They feem to have entered into
" a league not to difturb each others.tranquil-
" lity. The fea-lions occupy moft of the fea-
" coaft; the fea-bears take up their abode in
" the ifle; the fhags have poft in the higheft
" cliffs; the penguins fix their quarters where is
" the moft eafy communication to and from the
" fea; and the other birds chufe more retired
" places. We have feen all thefe animals mix
" together, like domeftic cattle and poultry in
" a farm yard, without one attempting to moleft
                                          " the

" the other. Nay, I have often obferved the
" eagles and vultures fitting in the hillocks
" among the fhags, without the latter, either
" young or old, being difturbed at their pre-
" fence. It may be afked how thefe birds of
" prey live? I fuppofe on the carcafes of feals,
" and birds which die by various caufes; and
" probably not a few, as they are fo nume-
" rous."

A Voyage towards the South Pole, &c.
By James Cooke. Vol. ii. p. 206.

NOTE [D], p. 19.

IT is the tendency of a fecond marriage to
weaken the ties of filial, as of parental love:
and this effect is by far more confpicuous in the
fecond marriage of a mother than of a father;
a circumftance which fuggefts a curious queftion
in the theory of moral fentiment, an ingenious
folution of which may be feen in the philofophy
of Hume.

Treatife of Hum. Nat. v. ii. p. 140.

Note [*E*], p. 21.

THE plan of domeſtic ſociety is various in
different ages and nations. In different
climates and ſituations it becomes more or leſs
expedient to controul the love of variety, and
natural the licentiouſneſs of deſire.

A community of wives was allowed in Sparta.
A latitude of the ſame kind was indulged at
Rome.   Such communities were found eſtabliſhed among the ancient Britons, and take
place among various tribes of Barbarians.   In
other caſes, the irkſome ſituation of fathers
under an impreſſion of a dubious progeny has
led to a ſyſtem of reſtraint, and prevention no
leſs barbarous than inhuman.   Some nations,
diſtruſtful of all the moral guardians of female
virtue, prevent by phyſical expedients the poſſibility of tranſgreſſion.   The modern Arabians
in particular, among whom jealouſy is the reigning paſſion, are guilty of a ſpecies of violence
too ſhocking for deſcription.

Polygamy,

Polygamy however, in fome form or other, appears to have been almoft univerfal. The moderation indeed of the ancient Germans is mentioned by Tacitus; yet among them a plurality of *wives* was not without example. Even a plurality of *hufbands*, according to Strabo, took place in certain provinces of the Medean empire : and fuch plurality is recognized in the Gentoo code.

The abolition therefore of polygamy has been reprefented by fome writers as a fort of fumptuary law, founded on the exigencies of civil fociety.

But againft one fpecies of polygamy the want of the afcertainment of the father forms an infuperable objection. Nor is it by any means clear that polygamy, in its more admiffible form, and how well foever regulated, is conducive to population or public profperity; and the near equality in the number of each fex, fufficiently arraigns the juftice of this eftablifhment. Where that proportion fubfifts, a community of wives, though defervedly exploded as tending to relax or to annihilate the paternal tie, is, perhaps, more defenfible than the exclufive poffeffion of a plurality. But fhould the proportion be in-

E   terrupted

terrupted or broken by peſtilence, by war, or
other ſignal calamity, a well ordered polygamy
might poſſibly ſerve as a temporary expedient
for repairing the depopulation of mankind.

On ſuch emergency it was allowed at Athens ;
and from a conviction, no doubt, of its propriety, Socrates and Euripides availed themſelves of the indulgence. But ſuch conjunctures
are rare; and an excluſive polygamy muſt in
general be regarded in a leſs favourable light,
as the moſt dangerous monopoly that ever
claimed the protection of government, and in
its origin and progreſs as an uſurpation of the
powerful and opulent on the equal pretenſions
of mankind.

Perhaps the liberty of *divorce* tended, at leaſt
in the more temperate climates, to reconcile all
ranks to a more equal plan.

The inſtitution of *ſingle marriages* accordingly
was in Greece as ancient as Cecrops, and was
adopted by the Romans as the moſt perfect
plan of domeſtic life. Yet even under this
inſtitution, the perpetuity of the marriage-union
may be vindicated on ſolid grounds: and a
riſing progeny, the offspring of mutual love,
tends

tends to confolidate the alliance, as well as to render its obligations indiffoluble. It is accordingly remarkable, that divorces, though permitted by law, were, during a period of five hundred years, unprecedented in the annals of Rome.

It is no lefs remarkable, according to the obfervation of a learned prelate *, that the number of divorces in the prefent reign equals the accumulated number upon record, in all preceding reigns, in the annals of England.

This decline of public manners is furely alarming, and calls, perhaps, for the interpofition of legiflative power. But it is feldom in the power of government to mend the morals of a people, while ill digefted attempts may ferve rather to haften corruption.

Whether it is poffible for the wifdom of a Britifh Parliament, to recal, in our age, the dignity of domeftic life, I pretend not to decide. Let it fuffice to obferve that, in the diffolute ages of antiquity, this liberty of divorce, authorized on fo flight pretences by the legiflation of Greece and Rome, and even tolerated under

* The Bifhop of Llandaff.

E 2   the

the Jewifh œconomy, became a fource of the moft odious corruption. The circumftances of the world called aloud for reformation. A latitude in this article was found alarming to the peace and order of fociety, and was finally reprobated and abolifhed by the maxims of our holy religion.

Upon the whole, it may be affirmed that the inftitution of marriage, more or lefs perfect in different countries, is regulated in the beft manner poffible, under the Chriftian fyftem. The liberty of divorce is dangerous, a community barbarous, and polygamy unjuft.

It may farther be obferved, that the laws of moft countries, relative to *inceft*, though not the immediate fuggeftions of inftinct, are founded on obvious views of expediency and public order. Inceft in the afcending and defcending lines is fo uniformly odious and fhocking, that the prohibition may be regarded as the unalterable and declared fenfe of mankind, wherever thefe relations are known. The inceftuous marriages of the Affyrians, Perfians, and fome others, which feem to militate againft this conclufion, are rightly afcribed to the dictates of a falfe religion, which is found, in fo many inftances,

inftances, to triumph over the cleareft maxims of reafon and morality.

There is no ground then to accufe fuch falutary regulations, or envying the unlimited indulgence of other times, to exclaim in the intemperate language of the poet,

> ——————Felices quibus *ifta* licent!
> ————humana malignas
> Cura dedit leges : & quod *natura* remittit
> Invida jura negant.
>
> OVID. L. 10.

NOTE [*F*], p. 22.

TACITUS, Plutarch, and others, bear teftimony to the honourable rank of the other fex among the ancient Gauls.—They are even faid to have conferred the fupreme judicature on their wives, fupplanted, however, in that function by an artful priefthood. The women were no lefs honoured among the ancient Britons. They were not only fuffered to vote in public affemblies, but raifed occafionally to the fovereignty of provinces, and even to the command of armies. Their importance among the ancient Germans, and in general under the

E 3   Gothic

Gothic conftitutions, is eftablifhed by a writer who has illuftrated the liberal genius of feudal affociations, and vindicated, in fome material points, the character of our remote anceftors *.

In feveral countries of Africa the women are ftill permitted to vote in public; and a multitude of fimilar examples might be drawn from the annals of uncivilized nations. But the † *Author of the Effay on the Hiftory of Civil Society*, in delineating the character of rude nations, prior to the eftablifhment of property, explains the facts alluded to fomewhat differently.

He admits, that children are confidered as pertaining to the mother, with little regard to defcent on the father's fide. He admits, that domeftic functions are committed to the women, that the property of the houfhold is vefted in them, and even that the hunter and the warrior are numbered as a part of their treafure; but contends, " that this fpecies of property is in " reality a mark of fubjection; not, fays he, " as fome writers allege, of their having ac- " quired the afcendant."

* See a View of Society in Europe, by G. Stewart, LL. D.
† Dr. Adam Ferguson.

But

But should we admit to this ingenious Author, that the occupations allotted for the women are accounted more inglorious than the toils of war, and would even be thought to sully and debase the character of the warrior or hero; yet such arrangements, without derogating from the prerogative of the superior sex, must render the condition of the inferior more eligible far than in several of the succeeding stages in civil society : " And if," to use the language of our Author, " in this tender, though unequal alliance, the affections of the heart prevent the severities practised on slaves; we have in the custom itself, as, perhaps, in many other instances, reason to prefer the first suggestions of nature to many of her after-refinements."

In such circumstances too the matrons, as the only ascertained parents of the rising generation, could not fail to command exclusively that respect and reverence which is the usual tribute of filial love. The due balance of domestic authority being maintained by the equal ascertainment of both parents, where the descent is dubious on one side, the balance must incline strongly to the other; and though it is scarcely credible that mankind ever carried their jealousy

of

of this authority fo far, as to undermine its foundations, by changing the children as foon as born; we may believe that uncertainty of defcent on the father's fide contributed to the importance at which the women arrived in Britain, in Gaul, in Sparta, and other ftates.

When it was obferved by one of another country to the wife of Leonidas, that at Sparta alone the women ruled the men, fhe replied, with becoming fpirit, " we are the only women who bring forth men."   .

The love of war and of women is combined, according to Ariftotle, in the character of nations.   And it muft be admitted, that a fpirit of gallantry, and a generous protection of the weaker fex, which form diftinguifhing features of the heroic age, are by no means unexercifed in the earlieft arrangements of the human fpecies.

The fair fex commanded more veneration among the ancient Celtic nations of Europe than among the Greeks and Romans, whom we are accuftomed to regard as the moft civilized

ized nations of antiquity. And their condition, though not to be envied, was lefs unhappy among the rude tribes in North America, than in the cultivated empires of Peru and Mexico, in other refpects the moft enlightened governments of the new hemifphere.

ESSAY II.

IN tracing the origin of arts and fciences, it is not uncommon to afcribe to the genius of a few fuperior minds, what arifes neceffarily out of the fyftem of man. The efforts of an individual are familiar to the eye. The efforts of the fpecies are more remote from fight, and often too deep for our refearches.

·The connexion, therefore, of events with an individual, is a more popular idea, while it gratifies an admiration and enthufiafm natural to the human mind. Hence the conduct of hiftorians, who defcribe the origin of nations. Hence

2   are

are celebrated among every people, the firſt
inventors of arts, the founders of ſociety,
and the inſtitutors of laws and government.

Such revolutions, however, in the condition of the world, are more juſtly reputed
the ſlow reſult of ſituations than of regular
deſign, and have, perhaps, leſs exerciſed
the talents of ſuperior genius, than thoſe
of mankind at large. *Uſages* there ſurely
are of mere arbitrary inſtitution; *inventions*
there ſurely are which originate with one
only, or with a few authors. But other
uſages and inventions as neceſſarily refer
themſelves to the multitude; nor ought
the caſual exertions of the former to be
confounded with the infallible attainments
of the ſpecies.

Under this precaution, then, let us introduce the queſtion concerning language. Is
language, it may be aſked, derived to us

at firſt from the happy invention of a few,
or to be regarded as an original accom-
pliſhment and inveſtiture of nature, or to
be attributed to ſome ſucceeding effort of
the human mind?

The ſuppoſed tranſition of the ſpecies
from ſilence to the free exerciſe of ſpeech,
were a tranſition indeed aſtoniſhing, and
might well ſeem diſproportioned to our intellectual abilities. Neither hiſtory nor
philoſophy are deciſive upon this point;
and religion, with peculiar wiſdom, refers
the attainment to a divine original. Suitable to this idea, language may be accounted in part *natural*, in part *artificial:*
in one view it is the work of providence,
in another it is the work of man. And
this diſpenſation of things is exactly conformable to the whole analogy of the
divine government. With reſpect to the
organs of ſpeech, what is there peculiar to
boaſt?

boaſt? The ſame external apparatus is common to us and to other animals. In both the workmanſhip is the ſame. In both are diſplayed the ſame mechanical laws. And in order to confer on them ſimilar endowments of ſpeech, nothing more ſeems neceſſary than the enlargement of their ideas, without any alteration of anatomical texture. In like manner, to diveſt, or to abridge mankind of theſe endowments, ſeems to imply only the degradation of the mental faculties, without any variation of external form.

It is not then ſuppoſed that the organs of man alone are capable of forming ſpeech. The voice of ſome animals is louder, and the voice of other animals is more melodious than his. Nor is the human ear alone ſuſceptible of ſuch impreſſions. Animals are often conſcious of the import, and even recognize the harmony of ſound. Thus

far

far there fubfifts a near equality. Vifible
figns are likewife poffeffed in common;
and language, in every fpecies, is the
power of maintaining focial intercourfe
among creatures of the fame order.

By the fame medium man is able to
converfe, in fome fort, with the brute
creation; and there the various tribes with
each other. But befides fome general figns
conftituted to preferve harmony and correfpondence among connected fyftems, there
are others of a more myfterious kind
deftined for the ufe and accommodation of
each particular clafs. In this fcience the
fagacity of the philofopher has hitherto
made no difcoveries. The myftery of animal correfpondence will, probably, be always hid; and it is often no more poffible
to defcend into the receffes of their intercourfe, than to open a communication with
a higher fyftem.

In

In the great scale of life, the intelligence
of some beings soars, perhaps, as high
above man as the objects of his understanding soar above animal life. Let us
then imagine a man, in some other planet,
to reside among a people of this exalted
character.

Instructed in the sounds of their language, as the more docile animals are
instructed to articulate ours, he might articulate too, but could acquire no more.
He might admire the magnificence of
sounds louder or more melodious than he
had heard before. But by reason of a dis-
similarity and disproportion of ideas, these
sounds could never conduct him to the
sense; and the secrets of such a people
would be as safe in his ears, as ours in the
ears of any of our domestic animals.

For the same reasons, if one of superior race were to drop into our world, our
language

language might be, in some respects, im-
penetrable even to his understanding, because destitute perhaps of some perceptions
essential to our meaner system.

Thus each order possesses something peculiar, which is denied to every other; and
it belongs to the author of the universe
alone to exhaust that immensity of knowledge which he has diffused in various
kind and proportion through the whole
circle of being.

Here is an arrangement of providence
coeval with the birth of things; and con-
sidering the similarity of organical texture,
the *taciturnity* of the other animals is a
problem to be accounted for, as well as the
loquacity of man.

Whence comes it that *he* alone so far
extends the original grant as almost to con-
sider it as his peculiar and exclusive privi-

F   lege?

lege? Between the lower claffes and him there fubfifts one important diftinction. They are formed ftationary; he progreffive. Had the exact meafure of his ideas, as of theirs, been at firft affigned, his language muft have ftood for ever as fixed and immutable as theirs. But time and mutual intercourfe prefenting new ideas, and the fcenes of life perpetually varying, the expreffion of language muft vary in the fame proportion; and in order to trace out its original, we muft go back to the ruder ages, and beginning with the early dawn, follow the gradual illuminations of the human mind.

Man, we may obferve, is at firft poffeffed of few ideas, and of ftill fewer defires. Abforbed in the prefent object of fenfe, he feldom indulges any train of reflexion on the paft; and cares not, by anxious anticipation, to antedate futurity.

All

.All his competitions with his fellows are rather exertions of body than trials of mind. He values himſelf on the command of the former, and is dextrous in the performance of its various functions. Too impatient for ſlow enterpriſe; too bold and impetuous for intrigue, he uſes the reſources of inſtinct, rather than the lights of the underſtanding; is ſcarce capable of abſtraction, and a ſtranger to all the combinations and connexions of ſyſtematic thought.

In this ſituation of the world there is no need for the details of language. The feelings of the heart break forth in viſible form; ſenſations glow in the countenance, and paſſions flaſh in the eye. Nor are theſe ſilent movements the only vehicles of ſocial intercourſe.

Prior to the contexture of language, and the uſe of arbitrary ſign, there is eſtabliſhed

F 2 a mechaa mechanical connexion between the feelings of the foul and the enunciation of found. The emotions of pleafure and pain, hope and fear, commiferation, forrow, defpair, indignation, contempt, joy, exultation, triumph, affume their tones; and independently of art, by an inexplicable mechanifm of nature, declare the purpofes of man to man. Thefe affociations are neither accidental nor equivocal; not formed by compact, or the effect of choice, but are parts of an original eftablifhment calculated, in the firft œconomy, for all the occafions of focial life. And happy furely, in one refpect, was this conftitution of things, when men were not only devoid of the inclination, but unfurnifhed with the means of deceit; and fentiment and expreffion were thus conjoined, by the indiffoluble ties of nature.

Such accents and exclamations compofe the firft elements of a rifing language. And

And in thefe diftant times, when artificial figns have fo far fupplanted the natural, *interjection* is a part of fpeech which retains its primeval character, is fcarce articulated in any tongue, and is exempted from arbitrary rule.

After the introduction of artificial figns, the tone and cadence of the natural were long retained; but thefe fell afterwards into difufe; and it became then the province of art to recal the accents of nature.

The perfection of eloquence is allowed to confift in fuperadding to fentiment and diction, all the emphafis of voice and gefture. And enunciation, or action, as it is called, is extolled by the moft approved judges of antiquity as the capital excellence.

The decifive judgment of Demofthenes is well known: and the Roman orator,

who

who records that judgment, expatiates himſelf in almoſt every page, on that comprehenſive language, which, independently of arbitrary appointment, addreſſes itſelf to all nations, and to every underſtanding *.

In a certain period of ſociety, there reigns a natural elocution, which the greateſt maſters afterwards are proud to imitate, and which art can ſo ſeldom ſupply. At firſt, the talent of the orator, as of the poet, is an inborn talent. Nor has Demoſthenes, or Tully, or Roſcius, or Garrick, in their moſt animated and admired performances, reached, perhaps, that vivacity and force which accompany the rude accents of mankind.

In the ſame original connexion of things reſides the expreſſion of muſic, or the irreſiſtible tendency of the modulations of

* Vide Cic. de Orat. L. 3. et paſſim.

found

found to ſtir and agitate the different paſſions [*A*]. Hence the aſtoniſhing effect aſcribed to muſic in ancient times, and the empire it ſtill maintains, in a peculiar manner, over rude and unpoliſhed nations.

A Writer *, who exhauſts on his favourite ſcience ſo much ingenuity and learning, has aſſigned indeed other cauſes for the empire of muſic among the ancients, beſides its intrinſic excellence [*B*].

I oppoſe not ſuch reſpectable authority. But though the ſcience of harmony is progreſſive; though *ſimultaneous harmony*, or muſic in parts, is entirely modern, yet the union of found and ſenſe is an original union; and the moſt wonderful effects of that union are prior to the age of refinement.

* Dr. Burney's Gen. Hiſt. of Muſic.

F 4 " The

" The recitative in mufic, according to the obfervation of an exquifite judge *, is only a more tuneable fpeaking ; it is a kind of profe in mufic; its beauty confifts in coming nearer nature, and improving the natural accents of words by more pathetic and emphatical tones." The fcale of mufic in different countries is the fame; and all the variety of its expreffion throughout the earth forms but fo many dialects of one univerfal language as unalterable as the human paffions.

Such caufes then, in the infancy of mankind, operating alone, or with little aid, feemed to fuperfede all motives to invention; while affairs, however, were gradually approaching towards a different ftage.

Next to the impulfes of appetite, and the focial paffions, the talent of *imitation* difplays its force. Nor is this talent the gift of heaven to man alone. He fhares

* Congreve.

it

it in common with the creatures below
him, fome of whom avail themfelves of
its exertions in the purfuit of their prey.
That even the mufical notes of birds are
not altogether innate, but rather acquired
by imitation, is a propofition fupported by
late obfervations. Yet in confequence of a
predilection, not eafily explained, fimilar
or kindred notes appear to be univerfally
characteriftic of the fame fpecies, varying
only in different regions of the globe, like
different dialects of the fame tongue. One
fpecies of birds excels in imitation, and in
a variety of note; another in the perfection of mufical organs; and hence, by
combining the peculiar excellencies of different fpecies, an ingenious naturalift has
fuggefted a method of improving upon the
mufic of the grove [C].

Among animals, however, the talent of
imitation occurs more rarely, or is limited
to a few performances, and thefe reforted

to

to as an expedient, rather than as an ultimate end.

But the performances of man are confpicuous, and various, and almoft without
bounds. He is prompted to imitation from
a love of the effect, and exclufive of all
reference to farther end, enters it into the
lift of his pleafures. Often this fecondary
pleafure exceeds the primary. And there
are few, I imagine, who would reject an
entertainment of this fort, on the fame
principle with Agefilaus of Sparta. When
invited to hear a performer who mimicked
the nightingale to great perfection, the
faftidious king replied, " I have heard the
" nightingale herfelf." The entertainment might be unworthy of a king; but it
was declined, on a principle that forms an
exception to the general tafte. And imitation may be juftly called the firft intellectual amufement congenial with our being: in confirmation of which we might
                                        appeal

appeal to the firſt eſſays of infancy, to the taſte for the imitative arts ſo predominant in youth, and to the earlieſt compoſitions of antiquity [D].

Man alone is capable of imitating every creature, while he is, if I may ſay ſo, him- ſelf a creature which no other can pretend to imitate. In the indulgence then of this talent, he adopts, as it were, every mode of inſtinct, and re-echoes every voice in the foreſt. Even ſtill life attracts his at- tention; and the application of the ſame talent to every ſubject, renders him a maſter in expreſſion, and ripens his genius while it exerciſes his mechanical powers.

Thus is he occupied in borrowing not only from his own ſpecies, but in tranſcrib- ing, for his amuſement, the appearances of the natural and of the animal world; in collecting materials, without knowing their importance, and in laying with an

active,

active, though undesigning hand, the foundations of all arts and sciences.

This imitative faculty operates so vigorously on the organs of speech, that in some cases sound in general seems to become an object of imitation, without any particular archetype. Hence the mechanical trials of children in the easier expressions, when their organs are incapable of other articulation. And hence the same sounds run uniformly through all languages, to denote either parent, to whom the earliest expressions are presumed to be addressed.

By such exertions are we rendered capable of indicating, by intelligible signs, the more striking and familiar objects. But to give an additional compass to the powers of speech was reserved for another principle allied to the former, and often undistinguished in its operations, which may be deno-

denominated the *analogical* faculty. A faculty which has vaft power in binding the affociations of thoughts, and in all the mental arrangements; but with whofe influence on language alone we are at prefent concerned.

Hitherto language confifted in the voice of inftinct, or was drawn by imitation from an actual fimilarity in the nature of things. *Now* analogical connexions fupply the place of real refemblance. *Now* inftinct borrows aid from *imagination*; and it is the weaknefs of this principle which impofes the law of filence, and excludes all poffibility of improvement in the animal world. Here commences the reign of invention, and here perhaps we fhould ftop, and draw the boundary of art and nature.

There is not an object that can prefent itfelf to the fenfes, or to the imagination, which

which the mind, by its analogical faculty, cannot affimilate to fomething antecedently in its poffeffion. By confequence, a term already appropriated, and in ufe, will, by no violent tranfition, be fhaped and adjufted to the new idea. And thus the divifion and compofition of the primary figns will conftitute relations in found, correfpondent with thofe relations, real or imaginary, which fubfift among the objects of human knowledge. Thus the language of the Chinefe confifts of a few words only, which, by a variation of tone merely, become the reprefentatives of all the ideas of that enlightened people.

This mode of proceeding is fo confpicuous in our firft attempts, that it is with reluctance children adopt a word altogether new, fo long as they can affimilate the object to any of their former acquaintance. And it is wonderful to obferve with what

prompti-

promptitude, facility, and apparent ingenuity, they can draw fuch various expreffion out of their little ftore. It is accordingly no illiberal entertainment in prefenting ftrange objects to their fight, to wait by
way of experiment for their own conclufions, and to caufe them to diftinguifh
each by names of their own invention [E].
This would be, perhaps, no improper
exercife in training their infant faculties;
and it feems to have been upon the fame
principle that the firft of mankind, at the
defire and with the approbation of his
Creator, was able to name fo readily all
the beafts of the field, and the fowls of
heaven.

Many fubfequent innovations in language may be traced up to the fame fource;
and figns apparently the moft arbitrary
are either the refult of fome more refined
connexion, or are feparated from their
primitives by a longer chain of analogy.

By

By this power the fame natural fign, befides its primary, admits of a fecondary, and even of various import; and what originally denoted an outward object, is by a certain fubtlety of apprehenfion tranf-ferred to the qualities of the mind [*F*]. Thus language becomes figurative; and, without any extenfion of the vocabulary, takes in the compafs of our intellectual ideas. It is this principle likewife which conducts the fame fign from the individual to the fpecies, and by the frequent application of it, on fimilar occafions, confers on it a larger and a larger import, till at laft it acquires a general acceptation, without any painful or laborious effort.

This procefs of the mind accounts for the generation of all the different parts of fpeech, as might be fhewn more particu-larly in the rife of that effential conftituent of language, which by reafon of its import-ance is denominated the *verb*.

Not

Not only are emotions of different kinds excited by the objects of fenfc, but the fame kind of emotion is wonderfully modified, according to the circumftances of its birth. How various, even in the favage breaft, are the modes of love! how various the emotion of fear!

Let us then fuppofe that the lion and the ferpent are confidered by the favage as the moft hoftile and formidable among animals. A certain fpecies of terror would be excited by the approach of the one; a different modification of the fame emotion would be excited by the approach of the other.

Now, in the firft ftage of language, the natural figns of thefe kindred emotions, it is prefumed, would be employed to indicate, and to diftinguifh the approach of thefe animals. In the mean while, let it be fuppofed that the other inhabitants of

G   the

the foreſt have received their names. In theſe circumſtances it is abundantly natural for the ſavage to join the term, indicating the dread of the lion or ſerpent, with a proper name, in order to notify the approach of any other offenſive creature. This term, by an eaſy extenſion, will be transferred from offenſive to other creatures; and hence by a gradual tranſition, even to inanimate objects, till it is charged at length with a general affirmation, and poſſeſſes all the power of the verb [G].

Such ſteps as theſe, we may believe, have led to the more regular combinations of ſound; and, under this aſpect of things, we may conceive language ſtrong indeed, and animated, but probably remaining long without much compaſs, or coherence, or order. It conſiſted chiefly of detached phraſe. And though every ſound formed not a complete ſentence, as at the beginning, yet the more artificial arrangements

were

were unknown. Thofe connective particles
which intimate the relations of thought
were not yet brought into exiftence; and
the relations themfelves were rather infi-
nuated to the underftanding than expreffed
in form. Nor is this abrupt mode of
expreffion unfuitable to the circumftances
of the fimple ages. Sentiment, as well as
its drefs, hung then extremely loofe; and
men were not accuftomed to a chain of
reafoning, or to any complex fyftem of
thought. Nor is it lefs conformable to
the experience of our early life, the trueft
perfpective, perhaps, in which to contemplate the rifing genius of mankind. In
the firft dialects of children, the particles
are but little attended to, if not totally
difregarded. They reject the texture of
artificial language, even while they adopt
its words, prefenting the capital objects in
immediate fucceffion, without the interven-
tion of terms which are of a more obfcure
and abftract original. It is the fame mode

G 2   of

of proceeding which is fo often obfervable in vehement fpeakers, who, in the hurry of declamation, or of paffion, have no leifure to attend to the rules of grammar, or logic. The language of paffion accordingly, which confifts of broken periods, has been happily imitated by the poets, and might be here illuftrated, were it neceffary, by examples from the greateft mafters, whofe prerogative it is to difpenfe in favour of nature with the eftablifhed rules of art.

It is alfo remarkable in all the ancient tongues, that the moft important diftinctions and relations of objects are indicated by an inflexion of the voice, or a flight variation of the fame found, without reforting fo often to the little engines, which fupport the modern fyftems.

Even this inflexion of voice is not always indifpenfable; and in the oriental tongues no inconveniency is perceived from the

want

want of the *genitive cafe*; though there is neither an inflexion, nor any intervening particle to fuggeft the relation.

Let it not then be imagined, that abftract confiderations have entered far into the firft formation of fpeech. Such laborious effort had been ill fuited to the genius and circumftances of the firft inventors; and even the *particles* themfelves, though of more doubtful origin, have crept into exiftence, without any fevere application of metaphyfical force.

Thofe talents alone exercifed by every human creature, in acquiring his firft language, have been exercifed by the original inftitutors. In both cafes the love of imitation is often the prime mover, without any farther defign. Taught by parents, children learn to utter found, to which afterwards they affix a meaning. Taught by inftinct, men utter found at the begin-

ning,

ning, which the underſtanding afterwards
renders more ſignificant. In both caſes,
the act of the underſtanding is poſterior to
a ſort of organical impulſe; and in both
caſes there ſeems to be leſs abſtraction
than is contended for in the ſchools of
philoſophy.

Is a man, for example, to be reputed
ignorant of the force of particles, becauſe
he is incapable to give a metaphyſical account of their origin ? And if without
metaphyſics he apprehends theſe particles,
why not invent them too ?

If we ſuppoſe but one of the moſt obvious
relations to be diſtinctly marked by any
particle, that particle will, as it were ſpon-
taneouſly, offer itſelf upon all ſimilar occaſions; and from the law of analogy will
be gradually extended in its ſignification,
until it includes under it a vaſt variety of
relation : for it is transferred from object
to

to object in the *concrete*, without any abftract confideration of its powers.

It is eafier for the mind to perceive refemblance, than to fpecify the minute differences of things.   Hence the fame particles are ufed to denote various relations,
without our attending to their fpecific
differences.   And hence thefe terms, in all
languages, are fo liable to be confounded,
and carry often a fort of vicarious import,
mutually participating of the fame powers.

When the analogy lofes itfelf in refinement, new particles are devifed, and in-
vefted with a different office.   And were
an ordinary man called upon to define the
prepofitions, or other little conftituents of
any modern tongue, without a certain preparation of his faculties, the anfwer with
regard to the greater number would be
indefinite, or evafive, or merely negative.
This particle, might he fay, differs in its

G 4   import

import from that other: that other from a
third. They feverally denote relations altogether diffimilar. It is eafier to fay what
they are not, than what they are.

Should a more explicit anfwer be required,
he refers to others more learned than himfelf, or involves himfelf in a labyrinth, in
which the primary conftructors of language
never were involved, and from which the
logician or the philologift can hardly extricate him. ".The particles, fays a * writer
in whom thefe characters are united, are
among all nations applied with fo great
latitude, that they are not eafily reducible
under any regular fcheme of application.
This difficulty is not lefs, nor, perhaps,
greater in Englifh than in any other language. I have laboured them with dili-
gence, I hope with fuccefs; fuch at
leaft as can be expected in a tafk, which
no man however learned or fagacious has
yet been able to perform [H]."

* Dr. S. Johnfon.

He

He muſt be born then with a texture of brain as ſtrong as that of *Johnſon*: he muſt be a *Hercules* in metaphyſics, who can declare, in their metaphyſical character, the full import of theſe elements of ſpeech.

Yet the relations of its own thoughts the mind clearly apprehends. The ſigns of theſe relations, when once inſtituted, it apprehends with equal eaſe. But theſe relations, clear as the light in the preſence of particular objects, in their abſence are involved in obſcurity.

The vulgar find little difficulty to apprehend the ſoul itſelf in an embodied ſtate; but it is reſerved for the philoſopher to apprehend its ſeparate and abſtract exiſt- ence. And as well might it be contended that this ſublime apprehenſion had, in every age, entered into the imagination of our forefathers, as that the nicer relations of thought had exhibited themſelves naked to the underſtanding, and received names

in

in artificial language, disjoined from the
other members which compose the body of
this complex machine.

With reason therefore we conclude, that
the laws of analogy, by one gentle and
uniform effect, superseding or alleviating the efforts of abstraction, permit language to advance towards its perfection
free of the embarrassments which seemed to
obstruct its progress.

In most speculations upon this subject,
there reigns a fundamental error. It consists in referring the rise of ideas and the
invention of language to a different æra,
as if a time had ever been when mankind
laboured for utterance, yet sought in
vain to open intellectual treasures, and
to be exonerated from the load of their
own conceptions. Under this impression
we are apt to imagine some great projectors
in an early age, balancing a regular plan
for the conveyance of sentiment, and the
establish-

eftablifhment of general intercourfe. In
fuch circumftances, indeed, they muft have
revolved in imagination all the fubtleties
of logic, and entered far into the fcience
of grammar, before its objects had any
exiftence. Profound abftraction and gene-
ralization muft have been conftantly exercifed; all the relations of thought canvaff-
ed with care, compared with accuracy,
and arranged with propriety, and with
order: a defign competent, perhaps, to
fuperior beings, but by no means compatible with the limited capacity of the
human mind. Now thefe difficulties and
incumbrances, in a great meafure, difappear, by contemplating ideas and language
as uniformly in clofe conjunction; and the
changes in the former, and the innovations
in the latter of the fame chronological
date.

A few ideas, in the ruder ages, are fub-
jected to expreffion with the fame facility,

as

as a greater number in fucceeding periods.
And hence fpeech, in all its different parts,
is already formed, when the vocabulary is
exceeding fcanty, and there is no variety
or abundance in any one clafs. Thus a
Grammar even of the Lapland tongue contains all the grammatical parts of fpeech *.
Hence too the eafe with which a language
is attained in infancy, or early youth, and
the difficulty attending it in maturer age.
When the idea and the fign are contemporary attainments, and coincide in their firft
impreffions, they take root together; and
ferve reciprocally the one to fuggeft the
other. But where this coincidence is want-
ing, it becomes more difficult, if not impoffible, for the mind to collect its naked
thoughts, and fubject them afterwards in
all their variety to the arbitrary impofitions
of language.

* See a Laplandifh Grammar, lately publifhed by Mr.
Leem, Profeffor of the Lapland tongue.

A more

A more equal œconomy, therefore, has been maintained by the direction of that principle of analogy to which we fo often refer; and the connexion is more eafily eftablifhed, when, from the fimplicity and uniformity of favage life, the fame figns return fo often; when the whole compafs of the vocabulary is exhaufted upon familiar objects, and almoft comprized in the hiftory of a day's adventures. Thus a vocabulary, confifting of about twenty words, is faid to be fufficient, in all their ordinary tranfactions, for the purpofes of fome favage nations.

Language then, conftructed with fuch fcanty materials, increafes with the experience and difcernment of mankind. On a more exact furvey, the mind difcriminates its objects, and breaks the fyftem of analogy by attending to the minute differences of things. As therefore the *analogical faculty* enlarges the fenfe of words, the *difcriminating*

nating faculty augments them in number. It breaks speech into smaller divisions, and bestows a copiousness on language by a more precise arrangement of the objects. Thus by the distribution of our ideas, as well as by the enlargement of the fund, language is constantly enriched; and its barrenness or fertility among a rising people may be always estimated by the number of the objects, and the accuracy with which they are classed.

At a time when utility was almost re-garded as the whole of beauty, and perspi-cuity was the sole aim of speech, nothing superfluous would ever be admitted there. Afterwards the coalition and interferences of different tribes confounded the simpli-city of the institution, by the admission of foreign, identical, and supernumerary terms. The love of novelty and variety established their currency: a species of luxury is indulged in the commerce of

3 words:

words.   Each fimple inftitution fuftained a
fhock from the collifion of contending
fyftems, and out of thefe jarrings there
arofe more copious and mixed eftablifhments.

By fuch caufes is language diverfified by
degrees, in its words, in its texture, and
in its idiom. What is at firft only a variety
of dialects, produces diftinct languages in
fucceeding generations. And after feparation from the fountain the differences
among them become more confiderable in
proportion to the length of their courfe.
Thus the Englifh, the French, and Italian
tongues have borrowed their vocabulary
from the Greeks and Romans, while in
their texture and idiom they are allied to
the Celtic and to the Hebrew, or claim a
very diftant original.

But the confideration of thefe differences
would carry us beyond the limit of the
prefent

present design, which permits us only to
touch on the gradations of a simple institution referring to those faculties of the
mind which appear principally concerned
in conducting its successive improvements.
In the execution of the enterprise the mind,
no doubt, has exerted collectively, at all
times, various powers; but these are exerted in unequal proportion, according to
the circumstances of the world; and the
order here assigned appeared to our judge-
ment most consonant to the probability of
things, to the experience of early life, and
to the genius and complexion of the ruder
ages.

By such efforts, or at least by efforts
competent to the abilities of every society
of mankind, some rude system is con-
structed on the foundations of nature.
The superstructure becomes vast and magnificent, like the conceptions of the human
mind; but that superstructure is the work
of

of ages, and is as complicated and various, in the different regions of the globe, as the modes of civil life, as the afpect of nature, and as the genius of arts and fciences.

Having therefore confidered fpeech in its lower forms, we proceed to enquire into thofe fuperior marks of refinement and art which conftitute the criterion of a polifhed tongue.

H

NOTES.

NOTE [*A*], p. 71.

THOUGH the modulations of found declare in general the feelings of the heart, mufic imitates the focial paffions with the happieft fuccefs. A diftinction which intimates the fociability and generofity of man, and is well illuftrated by Dr. Smith in the *Theory of moral Sentiment.*

" When mufic imitates the modulations of
" grief, or joy, it either actually infpires us
" with thofe paffions, or at leaft puts us in the
" mood which difpofes us to conceive them.
" But when it imitates the notes of anger, it
" infpires us with fear. Joy, grief, love, ad-
" miration, devotion, are all of them paffions
" which are naturally mufical. Their natural
" tones are all foft, clear, and melodious; and
" they naturally exprefs themfelves in periods
" which are diftinguifhed by regular paufes,
" and which upon that account are eafily adapt-
" ed

" ed to the regular returns of the correfpond-
" ing airs of a tune. The voice of anger,
" on the contrary, and of all the paffions
" which are akin to it, is harfh and difcord-
" ant. Its periods too are irregular, fome-
" times very long, fometimes very fhort, and
" diftinguifhed by no regular paufes. It is
" with difficulty therefore that mufic can imi-
" tate any of thofe paffions, and the mufic
" which does imitate them is not the moft
" agreeable. A whole entertainment may con-
" fift, without any impropriety, in the imitation
" of the focial and agreeable paffions. It would
" be a ftrange entertainment which confifted
" altogether of the imitations of hatred and
" refentment."

Part I. fect ii. ch. 3.

Note [B], p. 71.

PERHAPS the fimplicity of ancient mufic
contributed to its effect. Perhaps from its
union with poetry it derived its moft alluring
charms. Yet thefe arts may, on fome occafions,
encumber each other, and ought, in the opinion
of fome good judges, to hold a divided empire.
This is a problem in the hiftory of mufic which
an adept in the fcience is alone capable to de-

H 2 cide,

cide, and I am ready to adopt the opinion and language of Dr. Burney, that " mufic and " poetry, like man and wife, or other affo- " ciates, are beft afunder, if they cannot agree; " and, on many occafions, it were to be wifhed, " that the partnerfhip were amicably diffolved."

The danger at prefent feems to be, that mufic in preference to poetry, and *inftrumental* mufic in preference to *vocal*, to which it is fo far inferior, fhould ufurp an improper dominion in all the politer circles. An obfervation of Mr. *Gay* to Dr. *Swift*, in the year 1723, rela- tive to the fafhionable tafte of the metropolis, is now applicable in a much larger extent. " As for the reigning amufement of the town," fays he, " it is entirely mufic; real fiddles, " bafs viols, and hautboys; not poetical harps, " lyres, and reeds. There is nobody allowed " to fay *I fing*, but an Eunuch, or an *Italian* " woman. Every body is grown now as great " a judge of mufic as they were in your time " of poetry; and folks that could not diftin- " guifh one tune from another, now daily " difpute about the different ftyles of *Handel*, " *Bononcini*, and *Attilio*. People have now for- " got *Homer*, and *Virgil*, and *Cæfar*, or, at leaft, " they have loft their ranks; for in *London* and

" Weft-

" *Weſtminſter*, in all polite converſations, *Sene-*
" *ſino* is daily voted the greateſt man that ever
" lived." But without reflecting on the national
taſte, let it be ſufficient to obſerve, that muſic
is not the only imitative art, which, in the
progreſs of refinement, ceaſes to be ſo ſignificant.

N'eſt il pas ſingulier, ſays Monſ. l'Abbé
Reynal, que dans les premiers ages du monde,
& chez les ſauvages, *la danſe* ſoit un art d'imitation, & qu'elle ait perdu ce caractere dans
les pays policés, où elle ſemble reduite à une
certaine nombre de pas executés ſans action, ſans
ſujet, ſans conduite? Mais il en eſt des danſes
comme des langues: elles deviennent abſtraites,
ainſi que les idées dont elles ſont compoſées.

Tom. vi. p. 27.

Note [C], p. 73.

I Refer the reader to Experiments and Obſer-
vations on the ſinging of Birds, by the Hon.
Daines Barrington, inſerted in the Philoſophical
Tranſactions of the year 1773.

" Theſe experiments," ſays Mr. Barrington,
" may be ſaid to be uſeful to all thoſe who
H 3 " happen

" happen to be pleaſed with ſinging birds.
" Becauſe it is clear, that, by educating a bird
" under ſeveral ſorts, we may often make ſuch
" a mixture as to improve the notes which
" they would have learned in a wild ſtate.

" It reſults alſo from the experiment of the
" linnet being educated under the vengolina,
" that we may introduce the notes of Aſia,
" Africa, and America into our own woods;
" becauſe if that linnet had been ſet at liberty,
" the neſtlings of the next ſeaſon would have
" adhered to the vengolina ſong, who would
" again tranſmit it to their deſcendants."

The muſical notes of birds, if we believe
Lucretius, a naturaliſt as well as a poet, firſt
ſuggeſted to man the elements of a ſcience in
which he afterwards ſo far excels them. For
the notes of birds, however melodious, are not
only deſtitute of harmony, but deficient in expreſſion, which in muſic is the capital excellence.

Note [D], p. 75.

IT is, perhaps, not foreign from the ſubject
to obſerve, that men of genius, though no
poets or painters by profeſſion, ſo often diſcover,

cover, in early life, a pronenefs to the imitative arts, which yield to more ferious occupation in maturer years. Even the mafters themfelves, in the decline of life, no longer court the mufes with equal affiduity. It is then the poet, tranf- formed into the philofopher, abandons his for- mer walk——

Hinc itaque & verfus & cætera ludicra pono.

The Biography of the Englifh Poets, to which a writer of the firft rank in literature now calls the attention of the public, affords a variety of examples of this predilection in early life. Cowley and Milton, as well as Pope, " lifped in numbers." Cowley had read all Spenfer, while under twelve, had commenced a poet at thirteen, and an author at fifteen, when his *poetical bloffoms* appeared. In the *Comus* of Milton, a juvenile production, we behold the dawn of an immortal day.

The author of Gondibert compofed a poem on the death of Shakefpeare, at the age of ten.

Dr. Jortin was a poet in youth, and a critic in maturer age.

H 4 Lord

Lord Lanſdown compoſed moſt of his poetical pieces when a perfect child, the correction of which afforded employment to his riper years.

Voltaire commenced poet at twelve, compoſed the Henriade while under twenty-four, and his *Brutus*, which he regarded " comme ſa tragedie la plus fortement ecrite," at thirty-ſix.

The preſent *Imperial Laureat**, an appellation which his merit alone might almoſt extort from his contemporaries, is an aſtoniſhing inſtance of the premature inſpiration of the muſes. And not to multiply inſtances among foreign nations, the Poems aſcribed to Thomas Rowley, a ſecular prieſt of Briſtol, who flouriſhed in the fifteenth century, are probably the production of a youth who died Anno 1770, at the age of eighteen, a prodigy of genius; and who, in the opinion of no contemptible judge, would have proved the firſt of Engliſh poets, had he reached the full manhood of his days. " From his childhood," ſays Mr. Warton, " he " was fond of reading and writing verſes, and " ſome of his early compoſitions, which he " wrote without any deſign to deceive, have " been judged to be moſt aſtoniſhing produc- " tions by the firſt critic of the preſent age."

* Metaſtaſio.

Waller

Waller indeed is recorded a singular instance of a poet, who began late the exercise of a poetic talent. " At an age," says Lord Clarendon, " when other men used to give over writ-
" ing verses (for he was near thirty years of age
" when he first engaged himself in that exercise,
" at least that he was known to do so), he sur-
" prised the town with two or three pieces of
" that kind, as if a tenth muse had been newly
" born to cherish drooping poetry."

But this evidence is not conclusive; nor is the noble historian perfectly correct in point of fact. For the muse of Waller had even acquired a name in the twenty-fourth year of his age. It is reasonable, however, to expect that the more perfect performances of a great master will be of later date. A correct judgment is a quality so essential to great execution in the imitative arts, that, according to the Abbé du Bot, it is about the age of thirty that the greatest geniuses, whether in poetry or painting, have produced their master-pieces.

But to this Dryden is an eminent exception. His latest performances are the best. His fire, says Pope, like the sun's, shone clearest towards its setting. Addison adorns him with similar

4   praise;

praife; and he merited the following encomium
from the illuftrious patron of his declining age:

> Not all the blafts of time can do you wrong,
> Young fpite of age, in fpite of weaknefs ftrong;
> Time, like *Alcides*, ftrikes you to the ground;
> You, like *Antæus*, from each fall rebound.

Note [*E*], p. 79.

OMIAH, the Otaheitean, circumfcribed as a
child in the number of his ideas, though
in underftanding and in years a man, proceeded
on fimilar principles in the acquifition of the
Englifh tongue.

The butler he called king of the bottles,
Captain Fourneaux was king of the fhip, Lord
Sandwich was king of all the fhips. The whole
language of his own country exceeds not a
thoufand words.

Note [*F*], p. 80.

SUCH is the natural order of analogy in the
generation of fpeech. But the reverfe order,
where words expreffive of ideas purely intellectual, are transferred to corporeal objects, is
fome-

fometimes obfervable in a cultivated language; inftances of which are produced in *Melange de Literature par Monf. d'Alembert.*

NOTE [G], p. 82.

IN elucidating this part of fpeech, it has been well obferved by Dr. Smith, that " imper-
" fonal verbs, which exprefs in one word a
" complete event, which preferve in the ex-
" preffion, that perfect fimplicity and unity
" which there always is in the object and in the
" idea, and which fuppofe no abftraction or
" metaphyfical divifion of the event into its
" feveral conftituent members of fubject and
" attribute, would, in all probability, be the
" fpecies of verbs firft invented."

But afterwards, in the progrefs of language, by the divifion of every event into its metaphy-fical elements, imperfonal verbs difappear. In modern tongues, accordingly, they are unknown. Yet they make a figure in the languages of antiquity, and efpecially in the Hebrew, where the radical words, from which all others are derived, are traced up by grammarians to that original.

See Confiderations concerning the firft Formation of Languages, &c.

NOTE

Note [*H*], p. 88.

THE ill fuccefs of all former grammarians ancient and modern, has not intimidated a writer in the gloom and folitude of a prifon, from undertaking fo arduous a tafk.

See a letter to John Dunning, Efq; by Mr. Horne. In this letter the conjunctions of the Englifh tongue are traced up to a fource unobferved or unacknowledged by any grammarian. The fame analogy is prefumed to be univerfal; and conjunctions, according to this plan, no longer rank among the grammatical elements, but are derived in one uniform manner, in all languages, from the other parts of fpeech.

ESSAY III.

THE connexion of language and manners is an obvious connexion. They run parallel with each other, through different periods of their progrefs. Yet language, from various caufes, may arrive at a pitch of refinement, unauthorifed by the tone of public manners. And on the other hand, public manners may acquire a fuperior caft of refinement, which the language alone would not authorife us to expect.

So various and equivocal are the marks either of rudenefs or refinement in the language and manners of a people, that to form, on fuch fubjects, a confiftent theory, is no eafy tafk. In both cafes, however,

a man

a man of taſte and obſervation muſt feel
and recognize diſtinctions, though he were
unable to ſpecify them, or to aſſign with
preciſion the laws by which they are governed.

We have attempted to approach the common fountain of all languages, but pretend
not to purſue the meanders of their courſe.

Articulation, if not an univerſal attribute of human ſpeech, is an excellence at
which it ſoon arrives [*A*]. Of rudeneſs,
therefore, or refinement, this particular
can form no criterion. Language too, in
both extremes, may be ſubjected to rules
of ſyntax nearly ſimilar; and by conſe-
quence the principles of grammar will not
carry us far into the origin of theſe diſtinctions. Is there an appeal to the ear; ſome
diſtinction is perceived, and a rougher tone
and cadence are found to correſpond beſt
with the temper and manners of Barbarians.

At

At firſt *perſpicuity* is chiefly or alone
regarded. Nothing conducive to that end
is offenſive to the organ; but afterwards
perſpicuity is in part ſacrificed to ornament.
Some indulgence is ſhewn to the ear; and
its perceptions acquire refinement, as well
as all our other perceptions. Hence ariſes,
by infenſible gradations, a new ſyſtem of
ſounds.

Words fluctuate with the modes of life.
They are varied, or exterminated as harſh
and diſſonant, upon the ſame principle that
any mode or faſhion is varied or exterminated as rude and vulgar. And the prevalence of this principle ultimately tends
to the eſtabliſhment of a general diſtinction.
Hence the ſmoothneſs of the Ionic dialect,
rather than the roughneſs of the Doric,
recommends itſelf to a poliſhed age.

Peter the Great conſidered the *German*
as a ſmooth and harmonious tongue, and
ordered

ordered it as fuch to be ufed at Court. In proportion as the Court of Peterfburgh became more polifhed, the German was difcarded, and the French fubftituted in its room.

In general the fuperior refinement of the French eftablifhed its currency in all the politer circles of the North of Europe. And upon the fame principle the Greek, which had no charms for the Romans in the ruder ages of the republic, ravifhed the ears of imperial Rome,

Hoc fermone pavent; hoc iram, gaudia, curas,
Hoc cuncta effundunt animi fecreta.

Juv. Sat. vi.

In the production of the founds of language *climate* [B] is concerned, as well as the degrees of civilization. But this natural caufe operating upon manners alfo, and through that medium upon fpeech, its direct and fimple influence upon the organs ought

ought not to be confounded with its reflex and more complicated operations.

Climate, in both ways, may favour or obſtruct refinement in ſounds, or derive to them a peculiar character.

If the language of the Malais, a people, barbarous and fierce, is however rightly celebrated as the ſofteſt in * Aſia, the climate, in ſuch inſtances, by an irreſiſtible application to the organs, acts in oppoſition to manners, and controuls their natural tendency. If the jargon of the Hottentots is, on the other hand, the harſheſt jargon in the world, it ſeems an effect rather chargeable on manners with which the climate is not immediately concerned.

In periods, however, of equal refinement, the articulation and accents of the North

* Voyez Les Voyages d'un Philoſophe, par M. Le Poivre.

I are,

are, in our hemifphere, diftinguifhable from the articulation and accents of the fouthern regions. Inarticulate found is governed by fimilar rules, and a different ftyle and compofition in mufic are found beft accommodated to the genius of different nations.

The French mufic accordingly, as well as the Italian, is univerfally exploded among the Turks; and whether from the texture of their organs, or from climate, or from certain habitudes of life, poffeffes no power to ravifh their ears with harmony, or to intereft the paffions.

In general European mufic is difrelifhed, or exploded in the Eaft. " Your mufic," faid a native of Egypt to M. Niebuhr, " is a wild and offenfive noife which a ferious man can hardly endure." Nor is this an anomalous example. When Ifmenias, the greateft mafter in mufic at the Court of Macedon,

Macedon, was commanded to perform before the king of Scythia; the king [C] having heard the performance, far from acquiescing in the public admiration, swore that to *him* the neighing of a horse was more agreeable : so little acceptable to *Scythian* ears, and to a barbarous monarch, were the most admired compositions of the Greeks.

Even among nations of equal refinement there is to each appropriated a style in music resulting from local circumstances, or from certain peculiarities of character; and national music, because more intelligible, will ever be more acceptable than foreign [D], to the inhabitants of every country. Thus the same sounds, though in some respects intelligible to all, excite perceptions which are merely relative, and therefore variable with the mechanism of our organs, with the associations of fancy, and with the cultivation of taste. It is the same with words. Words adopted

I 2　　　　　　　　　　into

into language, in the age of barbarifm, and whofe harfhnefs then is either not difcernible, or not offenfive, will of courfe be relinquifhed, or abolifhed in a more difcerning and cultivated period. And by confequence, *fentences* conftructed with fuch different materials, though the vehicle of the fame ideas to the underftanding, will imprefs our organs with characteriftical and diftinct perceptions.

It is a remark of Voltaire, in celebrating the illuftrious founders of Helvetian liberty, that the difficulty of pronouncing fuch names had injured their fame with pofterity.

A fimilar remark might be formed with regard to certain fciences and arts, where technical terms abound, and a difcouragement arifes from the coarfenefs of the language in which they are delivered. Not to mention the ufelefs jargon of the fchools, grown

grown fo juftly offenfive to the public ear, the barbarifm of its fcientific terms proves in the prefent age, at leaft in the fafhionable world, rather unfriendly to the Linnæan fyftem. This naturalifts confefs. The late Mr. Gray, whofe mufical parts were fo delicate and correct, was fo ftruck with this deformity in a fyftem in other refpects fo worthy of admiration, as to have attempted to make the German Latin of Linnæus purely claffical *: a tafk which perhaps Gray alone was able to. perform. But though this fpecies of deformity may be an object of regret, faftidious furely, or rather to the laft degree fantaftical, is the tafte which can be diverted, by fuch frivolous confideration, from the ftudy of nature.

The fenfe of harmony in a well conftituted mind, difpenfes with its objects, in

* See Gray's Works by Mafon.

favour

favour of more liberal and manly indulgence. And in the expreſſion of ſound,
in the intimation it brings, in the ſentiments and feelings, which, independently
of arbitrary appointment, it calls up in the
human underſtanding, or impreſſes on the
human heart, conſiſts the chief importance
of thoſe modulations which prevail in different ſyſtems of language.

When the Emperor Charles the Fifth [E]
ſo pleaſantly characteriſed the ſeveral languages' of Europe, this general effect of
ſound alone exhauſted the criticiſm. He
inſinuated no other compariſon, nor en-
quired into their artificial fabric. The
criterion, however, of a poliſhed tongue
ſeems principally to reſide there.

Idiom and analogical texture preſent
conſiderations of far greater importance
than can be drawn from any general theory
of ſound.

After

After a language has arrived at confider-able refinement, there may be remarked in provincial phrafe, or in the variety of its dialects, the characteriftics of primitive barbarifm. In this variety, its alliance with manners cannot efcape the moft fuper-ficial obferver. For, in the progrefs of a ftate, the lower ranks often fall back; or at leaft not moving forward in exact pro-portion with their fuperiors, their lan-guage, like their manners, remains long nearly ftationary. The vulgar, accord-ingly, of the fame country, almoft as widely differ in their vocabulary from the more polifhed, as the more barbarous differ in theirs from the more polifhed nations; or as the fame language differs from itfelf in its fucceffive ftages. And from hence a prefumption arifes, that the diftinction in queftion lies not fo much in found, or in grammatical texture, as in the analogy of terms which, in different periods of fociety,

I 4

are

are engrafted on a different ſtock. At one
period there is a coarſeneſs and ruſticity
which governs the idioms, runs through
the etymology, and adheres to all the alluſions. At another period the alluſions
carry us more immediately and directly to
the arts of life. In circumſtances ſo diſſimilar, the vocabulary is extended in oppoſite lines, and purſues its progreſs through
a different ſeries of analogy.

Suitable to this tendency of things, the
rough, the boiſterous, and the loud, the
true repreſentatives of barbarians in a cultivated age, are peculiarly averſe from refinement in ſpeech, and diſcover an aptitude and predilection for vulgar alluſions.

Even when the accidents of birth and
fortune lead to its more poliſhed forms, it
is difficult for art to file off, in this reſpect,
the roughneſs of nature; and they relapſe
into

into barbarifms better adapted to their mode
of thinking, and to the conftitutional inde-
licacy of their moral frame. To perfons of
an oppofite defcription, the grofs allufions of
the vulgar are peculiarly offenfive. A reformation in this point is more or lefs the
aim of the civilifing part of fociety; till
at length the reigning propenfities of one
become reigning antipathies in another age.

The fyftem of allufions, therefore, the
courfe of etymology, or the *filiation* of
words, muft be variable, in every tongue,
with the manners, with the arts, with the
turn of thinking among mankind. And
befides thefe intrinfic differences, which
rife up fyftematically out of the prevailing
fcheme of thought, words acquire dignity
or meannefs from accidental combinations,
and even from the organs through which
they pafs. They are fanctified, if one
may fay fo, by venerable lips, or contract
a fort of ideal debafement in the mouths of

4   the

the vulgar. And hence the poets of all nations, the firſt refiners of the elements of ſpeech, depart the fartheſt from vulgar phraſe, and even affeƈt a dialeƈt of their own, conſecrated in a peculiar manner to the muſes [F].

Such cauſes direƈtly tend to diſcriminate languages, and to fix the degrees of their refinement.

But refinement in language, as in manners, may be exceſſive, or ill governed. And comparative excellence is by no means included in comparative refinement [G].

Language, in its earlier forms, has been taxed with an obſcurity, from which it is afterwards exempt. This obſcurity, which reigns in ſome degree in all the languages of antiquity, has been more particularly objeƈted to thoſe of the Eaſt. It ſeems

princi-

principally to arife from the want of thofe connective particles whofe introduction is of a later date. And from hence it fhould feem that *perfpicuity* is a growing virtue. But the criticifm, if not deftitute of foundation, muft be confined, in a great degree, to written compofition. For, in the act of fpeaking, the fuperior vivacity, which accompanies a rude tongue, often fuperfedes the occafion of particles, or fcorns their aid. If then particles, in the fullnefs of their dominion, give only to *perfpicuity* what an inferior animation takes away, there is upon the whole no abfolute gain : and according as you fix the proportion, you refer the virtue to rude or cultivated fpeech.

Without inftituting a minute comparifon, it may in general be maintained, that the great excellence of a rude tongue confifts, if not in *perfpicuity*, at leaft in *viva-*

city

city and *strength*. In thefe modes of excellence our moſt remote progenitors far ſurpaſſed us. And the advantages of a cultivated tongue, when oppoſed to thefe, will confiſt chiefly in copiouſneſs of expreſſion, in the grace of alluſion, and in the combination of more melodious ſound.

An entire union of theſe qualities, with thofe others, would conſtitute the utmoſt perfection. But the exiſtence of the former, in an eminent degree, is rather incompatible with the latter; and confequently there is a certain point of refinement from which all languages begin to decline [*H*].

In forming a particular eſtimate, the inherent advantages and difadvantages of grammatical texture would alfo deſerve attention. It is the genius of ſome to admit of inflexion, and confequently of tranſpoſition, and a vaſt latitude of arrangement.

ment. Others, circumfcribed by particles, admit of no variety of order.

The one fyftem is more fertile of harmony and elegance, and even of ftrength; and by operating more fuccefsfully on the imagination, feems better adapted to the purpofes of eloquence and polite literature. The other fyftem, more allied to perfpicuity and precifion, is, on that account, more approved by the underftanding as a commodious vehicle for philofophy and the fciences. Any greater latitude of arrangement, than that permitted in the Greek and Latin, might probably be deftructive of perfpicuity. Any clofer confinement, than that required in the French and Italian, might be deftructive of elegance and force. In perfpicuity, the Englifh tongue is perhaps fuperior both to the Greek and Latin, while it falls confiderably fhort of the French. In elegance and force it is more

perfect

perfect than the French, while infinitely inferior to the Greek and Latin.

The German is an example of a language which admits of large transposition, while custom exacts much uniformity in the arrangement of words. Should the Germans then ever arrive at that elegance and taste which distinguished the politer ages of Greece and Rome, their writers would indulge in a variety of arrangement hitherto unprecedented, and which, though not repugnant to the fundamentals of their grammar, must wait the slow variation of idiom, the sanction of custom and established use.

Quem penes arbitrium est, & jus, & norma loquendi.

Such innovations, however, would be justly numbered among the ornaments of speech, and the refinements of a polished age. And other languages more melodiously dioufly conftructed, equally adorned, and fufceptible, perhaps, in other refpects of fuperior refinements, may be debarred, by the fundamental laws and conftitution of their grammar, from fuch eventual tranfitions.

But the critical examination of fuch particulars, or of the comparative excellence of ancient and modern tongues, belongs to the grammarian, or philologift, not to a writer who looks through their province into the progrefs of manners, and the viciffitude of civil life.

NOTES.

NOTE [*A*], p. 110.

THE language of the Hottentots, though not absolutely destitute of articulation, is, however, defective in this quality: And the language of the Troglodytes, a savage people, who subsisted in ancient Egypt, resembled, according to Herodotus, the shrieking of bats, and consisted of no articulate sounds. But in this instance, as in that of the Hottentots, and other savage nations, it is probable there is not a total absence of the quality, but only a more imperfect articulation, which requires some acquaintance with the language to render it palpable to sense.

NOTE [*B*], p. 112.

THE celebrated Signora Gabrieli, whose power of voice is so various and bewitching, is conscious of the irresistible influence of

physical

physical causes on her exertions. They disarm her occasionally of the power to excel, and account for that reluctance to perform, which is generally ascribed to caprice alone.

See Brydone's Tour.

NOTE [C], p. 115.

THE anecdote of Atheas king of Scythia is thus related by Plutarch:

'Ατεας———ισμηνιαν δε; τον αριστον αυλητην, λαβων, αιχμαλωτον, εκελευσεν αυλησαι: θαυμαζοντων δε των αλλων, αυτος ωμοσεν ηδιον ακυειν τε ιππε χρεμετιζοντος.

Plut. in Apophth.

It may even be questioned, whether the accomplished king of Macedon himself, though susceptible of musical gratification beyond the reach of a Scythian, had a full relish of the performances of the great master he affected to admire. But it was the policy of Philip to countenance at his court, a degree of refinement in the elegant and polite arts, which was little adapted to the circumstances of Macedon, though highly worthy of a prince who had annexed his kingdom to the Hellenic body, and

K   aspired

aſpired to the ſovereignty of nations highly civilized.

The Macedonians held a ſort of middle ſtation between the Grecian and Barbarian world. Rude, when compared with the Greeks; cultivated and refined, when compared with the Scythian nations.

Note [D], p. 115.

THOUGH muſical expreſſion is certainly relative to the peculiar ideas of a people, it cannot hence be inferred, that there is no ground of abſolute preference in judging of the muſic of nations. All languages, in their peculiar idioms, have ſuch a reference, yet a judgment may be formed concerning their comparative perfection. But to inſtitute ſuch compariſon belongs not to the crowd.

" The admiration," ſays a late popular writer,
" pretended to be given to foreign muſic in
" Britain is, in general, deſpicable affectation.
" In Italy we ſee the natives tranſported at the
" opera with all that variety of delight and
" paſſion which the compoſer intended to pro-
" duce. The ſame opera in England is ſeen
                                    " with

I

" with the moſt remarkable liſtleſſneſs and in-
" attention. It can raiſe no paſſion in the
" audience, becauſe they do not underſtand the
" language in which it is written."

The ſame writer, after enumerating ſeveral
cauſes which conferred pre-eminence on the
muſic of the ancients, proceeds to obſerve, " That
" if we were to recover the muſic which once
" had ſo much power in the early periods of the
" Greek ſtates, it might have no ſuch charms
" for modern ears as ſome great admirers of
" antiquity imagine."

Gregory's Comparative View.

The extent of theſe charms, we will preſume
to add, even for the ears of Greeks, is magnified beyond the truth. It can hardly be imagined, that their muſical education was eſſential to
public morals, or to the frame of their governments; though it might contribute, in ſome
degree, to ſway the genius of the youth, to
counterbalance the tendency of their gymnaſtic
exerciſes, and to heighten the ſenſibilities of that
refined and ingenious people.

NOTE

NOTE [*E*], p. 118.

FRANCESE ad un amico—Tudeſco al ſuo
cavallo—Italiano alla ſua ſignora—Spa-
gnuolo a Dio—Ingleſe a gli uccelli.

This apothegm, like an imperial edict, has
been rung, for above two centuries, in the ears
of Europe. Though rather pleaſant than ſe-
rious, it intimates from high authority the general effects of ſound. Serious criticiſm, on the
ſtructure of the European languages, leads to
more important diſtinctions, founded in the di-
verſity of national character.

" It is certain," ſays Addiſon, " that the
" light talkative genius of the French has not
" a little infected their tongue, which might
" be ſhewn by many inſtances; as the genius
" of the Italians, which is ſo much addicted to
" muſic and ceremony, has moulded all their
" words and phraſes to thoſe particular uſes.
" The ſtatelineſs and gravity of the Spaniards
" ſhews itſelf to perfection, in the ſolemnity of
" their language; and the blunt, honeſt humour
" of the Germans ſounds better in the rough-
                                    " neſs

" nefs of the high Dutch, than it would in a
" politer tongue."

Spectator, No. 135.

Note [F], p. 122.

THE embellifhment of a poetic dialect is
eminently confpicuous in the Greek and
Latin ; the languages ancient and modern moſt
eminent for every fpecies of refinement.

Whatever theory is embraced concerning the
origin of this dialect among the Greeks, the
advantages hence derived to the Greek mufe are
univerfally acknowledged. And the advantages
derived to the Italian mufe, from the fame fountain, are thus defcribed by Mr. Addifon in his
Remarks on Italy.

" The Italian poets, befides the celebrated
" fmoothnefs of their tongue, have a particular
" advantage above the writers of other na-
" tions in the difference of their poetical and
" profe language. There are indeed fets of
" phrafes that in all countries are peculiar to
" the poets ; but, among the Italians, there
" are not only fentences, but a multitude

K 3 " of

" of particular words that never enter into
" common difcourfe. They have fuch a dif-
" ferent turn and polifhing for poetical ufe,
" that they drop feveral of their letters, and
" appear in another form when they come to
" be arranged in verfe. For this reafon, the Ita-
" lian opera feldom finks into a poornefs of
" language, but amidft all the meannefs, and
" familiarity of the thoughts, has fomething
" beautiful and fonorous in the expreffion.
" Without this natural advantage of the tongue,
" their prefent poetry would appear wretchedly
" low and vulgar, notwithftanding the many
" ftrained allegories that are fo much in ufe
" amongft the writers of this nation."

Thus far Mr. Addifon. Suitable to the defign of this note, it may farther be obferved,
that the Provençal tongue, embellifhed by the
happy genius of the Troubadours, was, during a period of two centuries, the moft approved of any in Europe. It was the forming
hand of Dantè, that firft gave fo fine a polifh
to the Italian as rendered it fuperior to the Provençal, at a time when the Spanifh and French
were emerging more flowly from barbarifm. "
See Millot's Hiftory of the Troubadours.

The

The English tongue cannot indeed boaft of a poetic dialect of equal advantage with that of the Greek or Italian, yet is it not unacquainted with a fimilar fpecies of refinement.   The merit of fuch refinement is eminently Dryden's, who felected, with peculiar delicacy, fo many flow-ing and fonorous words, and appropriated them exclufively to the mufes.

" There was," fays his biographer and critic, " before the time of Dryden, no poetical dic-" tion, no fyftem of words at once refined from " the groffnefs of domeftic ufe, and free from " the harfhnefs of terms appropriated to parti-" cular arts.   Words too familiar or too re-" mote, defeat the purpofe of a poet.   From " thofe founds which we hear on fmall or " coarfe occafions, we do not eafily receive " ftrong impreffions or delightful images; and " words to which we are nearly ftrangers, when-" ever they occur, draw that attention on them-" felves, which they fhould convey to things.

" Thofe happy combinations of words, which " diftinguifh poetry from profe, had been rarely " attempted; we had few elegancies or flowers " of fpeech; the rofes had not yet been plucked

K 4   " from

" from the bramble, or different colours had
" not been joined to enliven one another."

Waller and Denham, it will readily be owned
by every cultivator of Englifh literature, claim
on the fame account a due proportion of praife.
But Dryden, certainly, has eclipfed their fame.

Waller was fmooth ; but Dryden taught to join }
The varying verfe, the full refounding line,
The long majeftic march, and energy divine.

NOTE [G], p. 122.

THE fimple and original qualities of ftyle,
confidered as an object to the underftanding, the imagination, the paffions, and the ear,
are reduced by Dr. *Campbel, in the Philofophy of
Rhetoric,* to five, *perfpicuity, vivacity, elegance,
animation,* and *mufic.*

If of thefe qualities perfpicuity is, as it furely
is, the moft effential, the aptitude of a language
to promote perfpicuity, would feem to conftitute
its chief perfection. But we may apply, perhaps, to perfpicuity, which is the firft end of
fpeech, what is applicable to fome of the moral
virtues,

virtues. The abfence of the virtue implies the moſt palpable defect; its preſence is no capital excellence.

Beſides, the caſes of ſtyle and of a language are not exactly parallel. In judging of the one, we pronounce on the execution; in judging of the other, rather on the materials. The archi- tect may not always be reſponſible for the ma- terials with which he builds. A language full of perſpicuity, within a narrow province, may, from the ſcantineſs of the vocabulary, be with- out variety, or compaſs, or extent.

As to the analyſis of ſtyle, it is foreign to this diſcuſſion. But if ſo curious a ſubject ſhould appear intereſting to the reader, we can refer him with pleaſure to the work above mentioned, which enters into minute as well as important diſtinctions, and which entitles its author to no inferior rank among the critics and metaphyſicians of the preſent age.

NOTE

Note [H], p. 124.

WHEN a language has touched the higheſt point of attainable perfection, it is open to corruption from various ſources, which no human ſagacity is able fully to explore.

It can be ſhewn from the doctrine of combinations, that it is poſſible, in the nature of things, for a language to *exhauſt itſelf*, ſo as to be utterly incapable of preſenting any *new* idea to the human underſtanding.

In any ſyſtem of words, the various combinations, and combination of combinations, cannot be infinite. But though not *infinite*, they are, it muſt be owned, *indefinite*; and therefore, the ſuppoſition we have made, is barely poſſible in the conception of the mind. Something, however, actually approaching to this takes place, to a certain degree, in a highly cultivated tóngue, and is a principal cauſe of its decline.

Modes of ſpeech, the moſt elegant and adorned, by returning often upon the ear, are
liable

liable to be anticipated, or ceafe to afford their wonted gratification. To aim therefore at new, though inferior forms of excellence, becomes an object in an age of refinement. Words of fingular fabric, foreign idioms, and combinations lefs familiar to the public ear, are fought after with avidity. The genius of the language is tortured; and the love of novelty and variety produces a conftant deviation from the pureft models.

The corruption arifing from this principle, was realized among the Romans after the Auguftan age, and begins perhaps to be realized in the prefent period of Englifh literature.

E S S A Y IV.

OF THE CRITERION OF CIVILIZED MANNERS.

THE epithets *barbarous* and *civilifed* occur fo frequently in converfation and in books, that whoever employs his thoughts in contemplation of the manners and hiftory of mankind, will have occafion to confider, with fome attention, both what ideas thefe words are commonly meant to convey, and in what fenfe they ought to be employed by the hiftorian, and moral philofopher.

It is of fome importance furely, in every difcuffion relative to human affairs, to have afcertained before-hand what are thofe qualities in the manners and characters of

different

different nations, which, according to the
eſtimation of reaſon, after an impartial ſurvey of mankind, as they are and have been,
may juſtify the impoſition of names imply-
ing almoſt unlimited cenſure or applauſe.

Perhaps, on examination, it will not
appear that any ſimple criterion of civilization and barbarity, taken either from
laws, or manners, or any other circumſtance in human affairs, can be fixed upon,
as ariſing from the general uſe which is
made of theſe terms, and fitted to explain
their application in particular caſes.

That civilization ſo highly extolled, is
plainly underſtood by its admirers to be
ſomewhat of a mixed and complicated nature, comprehending various conſtituent
parts, ſome eſſential to its very exiſtence,
ſome only acceſſory and ornamental. In
the total abſence of the former of theſe,
Barbarity,

Barbarity, according to the general acceptation of the word, feems to be underftood to confift.

Warm and fteady affections in private
life, an honourable fidelity to engagements,
whether exprefs or implied, the order of
internal laws, equity and humanity in
their conduct toward ftrangers, and foreign nations, will be infifted upon by all
as effential to the character of a civilized
people. The fciences, and fine arts,
though not indifpenfably effential, muft be
efteemed very requifite: yet is not their
influence exempted from fome uncertainty
and fufpicion.

The cultivation of real fcience, the
love and ftudy of the fine arts, while
uncorrupted, add, no doubt, to the po-
litenefs, and improve the enjoyments of
civilized

civilized nations; but an attachment to false sciences (several of which, like astrology and magic, unsuspected while they flourish, have prevailed, and perhaps prevail), or a passion for spurious and grotesque imitations of the fine arts, as pantomimes, puppet-shows, masquerades, or the laboured decoration of gardens and parterres, cannot improve, and may degrade and impair the just estimation of those nations by whom they are cherished.

The vulgar and commercial arts, subservient to the plenty, accommodation, and elegance of ordinary life, seem almost of an indifferent nature.

Although by these the manners of civilized nations may be embellished, yet the highest degrees of generous virtue, and the truest politeness of mind, may be found among nations to whom these arts are almost totally unknown.

If

If this be a full enumeration of the qualities which, in the general fenfe of mankind, are underftood to conftitute civilized manners, and a juft account of their refpective importance; it deferves to be adverted to, that no nation has ever poffeffed them all in their higheft excellence, nor has any fubfifted as a people (fhort periods of convulfion and anarchy excepted) without a very confiderable degree of one or more of thofe which are to be accounted moft effential.

Were it not then better to fet afide from correct reafoning the too general terms of *barbarous* and *civilized*, fubftituting in their room expreffions of more definite cenfure and approbation?

Indeed the common acceptation of thefe words is founded upon a very general, but very falfe and partial opinion of the ftate of mankind. It fup-

L   pofes

pofes that the difference between one
nation and another may be prodigioufly
great; that fome happy and diftinguifhed
tribes of men are, in all refpects, generous,
liberal, refined, and humane ; while others,
from their hard fate, or their perverfenefs,
remain in all refpects illiberal, mifchievous,
and rude.

This general fuppofition with regard to
the condition of human nature, is implied
in that opinion of their own fuperiority
over other nations which Europeans are
prone to entertain : a fuperiority which,
like that affumed by the Greeks, the Romans, and the Chinefe, is fuppofed by
thofe who claim it to be abfolute and immenfe ; yet, if brought to the ftandard of
virtue and felicity, it may appear very
inconfiderable in refpect of the populous
Afiatic nations, who have flourifhed long
under extenfive monarchies, and not very
great in refpect even of the fimpleft and
rudeft

rudeft race of men inhabiting the frozen
fhores of Greenland, or placed beneath the
fervour of a vertical fun, along the Guinea
coaft, or on the Banks of the Orinoco.

It ought to be fuppofed that, if other
nations were as far inferior to us, as we
are willing to imagine, their condition
would evidently tend to decay and extermination. With regard to the inferior
orders of being, both animal and vegetable, it feems to be a law of nature, that,
wherever they cannot attain, in fome very
confiderable degree, the honours, if I may
fo fpeak, and the emoluments of their
exiftence, there they gradually decline, and
at laft ceafe to exift at all. Is man an exception from the general law? or may it
not rather be believed, that, wherever any
tribes of mankind fubfift, and do not manifeftly decay and haften to extermination,
there, though appearances belie it, they
muft have attained a meafure of worth

and

and of felicity not much inferior to that which the moſt admired nations have actually attained ?

The opinions of the vulgar ſuggeſted by inſtinctive propenſities, not formed by reaſoning, always aſcribe to the progreſs of ſcience and of art, wherever they have once apprehended the idea of this progreſs, a ſuperiority of the moſt deciſive kind, in all that is fortunate and deſirable in the lot of man. But ſpeculative reaſoners are not wholly agreed on this head.

The greater number indeed have embraced, and by their eloquence they illuſtrate and enforce, this opinion ſo natural to the crowd, and, with them, they extol this progreſs as eſſential to the very exiſtence of the human character.

But of late a few *, not inferior in ſagacity to any, and more inquiſitive per

* Rouſſeau, and thoſe who have embraced his opinions.

haps,

haps, in this refearch, than thofe who have followed the generally received opinion, have found reafon to decry this progrefs as the fertile fource of corruption, debafement and infelicity.

Between thefe oppofite opinions the truth, as in many other cafes, will probably be found. The beneficial influence of this progrefs is real, yet far inferior to what the panegyrifts of fcience and art have reprefented it to be, and juft barely enough to reward that continual purfuit which it folicits from every nation once engaged in this career.

It will not however follow, if the condition of the moft improved and refined nations be admitted very little to exccl in felicity or worth the fimpleft and rudeft tribes of men, that the inducements to further progrefs in purfuit of improvement are taken away, or indeed diminifhed.

To

To nations of men, as to individuals, it happens often, that they are allured by the fplendor of a diftant object, to purfue it with more ardour than it appears on attainment to have deferved. They are then apt to complain of fallacious appearances, and to wonder that the fyftem, of which they are a part, fhould expofe them to fuch delufions. But though their induftry may have been roufed and excited by a certain degree of delufive fplendor, without the charms of which it might not have been awakened at all, they are never cheated of its proper reward.

Some real good, however inferior to that exhibited, or different from it, is generally obtained at the clofe of every purfuit; and whatever may appear deficient then, has been before enjoyed in detail, as it accompanied the progrefs of their endeavours.

Were

Were indeed both the progreffive reward of well-directed induftry, and that
which is obtained at the termination of its
endeavours, much inferior to their ufual
amount, one powerful reafon would ftill remain to impel mankind to the purfuit of
every attainable object, and to make them
afpire after every apparent improvement
of their actual condition, whatever it may
be.

———— Omnia fatis
In pejus ruere, ac retro fublapfa referri,
Ni vis humana————

The filent courfe of time is continually
taking away from that which we poffefs,
and from the high perfection of whatever
we have cultivated and refined. Nothing
ever ftands ftill. If progrefs is not made,
we muft decline from the good ftate already
attained, and as it is fcarcely ever in our
power to replace the work of time and
of chance in thofe very refpects in which

L 4 they

they have impaired our condition, we
ought to endeavour to compenfate thefe in-
evitable loffes, by the acquifition of thofe
other advantages and augmentations of good,
which the fame courfe of things brings
forward to our view, and feems to prefent
to us as the object of reafonable defire.

ESSAY V.

THE philofopher, who ftudies human nature in the clofet, will be
aftonifhed when he looks abroad into
life, and examines, by his theory, the
conduct of mankind.

Yet to him who, in the courfe of obfervation, and in the commerce of active life,
has learned to make no ferious appeals to
his own conftitution, the hiftory of the
world will be no lefs dark and myfterious.

The one is deficient in experience, the
other in reflexion; and both alike unqua-
lified

lified to judge confiftently of the human character.

Had there reigned from the beginning an exact fimilarity among men, laws had been unneceffary, and government without all foundation. A wide diffimilarity, on the other hand, muft have indifpofed them for fociety, and rendered them incongruous parts of the fame fyftem.

Diftinctions then there are, and ought to be. But thefe, at firft few and inconfiderable, have grown immenfe in the revolutions of time ; and the natural hiftory of the fpecies is fcarce able to folve the appearances in civil life.

The operation of climate, in the production of thefe appearances, feems to have been magnified by the Greeks and Romans. The genius of the Afiatics was fuppofed to difappear in the climates of
Europe,

Europe, and the genius of Europe to eva-
porate in the climates of Afia. Thus the
genius of the human mind feemed to
fluctuate with every migration, and to gra-
vitate to the foil [*A*].

Mechanical and local caufes, which, in
fome refpects, fo vifibly predominate, the
imagination invefts with a dominion that
reaches the very effence of our frame.
Hence the mutual contempt of nations.
Hence the rank which Europe, at this day,
ufurps over all the communities of mankind.

She affects to move in another orbit from
the reft of the fpecies. She is even offend-
ed with the idea of a common defcent; and
rather than acknowledge her anceftors to
have been co-ordinate only to other races
of Barbarians, and in parallel circumftances, fhe breaks the unity of the fyftem,
and, by imagining fpecific differences among
men, precludes or abrogates their common
claims.

According

According to this theory, the oppreſſion or extermination of a meaner race, will no longer be ſo ſhocking to humanity. Their diſtreſſes will not call upon us ſo loudly for relief. And public morality, and the laws of nations, will be confined to a few regions peopled with this more exalted ſpecies of mankind.

Upon the diſcovery of America, doubts were entertained whether the natives of that country ought not to be accounted a race of the Ourang Outangs. But the infallible ediᴅ of a Roman pontiff ſoon eſtabliſhed their doubtful pedigree [B]; and our right of dominion, in both hemiſpheres, was aſſerted, on other pretences, by the caſuiſts of thoſe days.

The inveſtiture of America was conferred on Ferdinand and Iſabella by Pope Alexander the Sixth.

In

In general all countries difcovered to the weft of a meridian line, were by this pope affigned to the Spaniards, as all difcovered to the eaft of this line were declared, by the fame authority, to be vefted in the Portuguefe.

It became accordingly a queftion after-wards between the two crowns of Spain and Portugal, to which of them the Mo-lucca Iflands fhould belong. For it had not occurred to this arbiter of the rights of kings, that the grants were as non-fenfical as unjuft; and that the eaftern and weftern navigators might poffibly inter-fere in taking poffeffion of their refpective allotments. But the court of Rome, which authorifed fo abfurd a partition of empire, vindicated, during another pontificate, the honours of the Indian race. The thunder of the Vatican was heard, for once, on the fide of humanity; and Europe, in the fixteenth century, was permitted only to

ufurp

uſurp the ſovereignty, not to inſult the
pedigree, of nations.

The theory, then, we have mentioned,
is, in its utmoſt extent, of more modern
invention. But the opinions which lead
to it are of high antiquity; and, being
congenial with the paſſions of a divided
world, have reſiſted the experience of ages.
There is ſcarce any folly or vice, ſays a
late author *, more epidemical among
the ſons of men, than that ridiculous and
hurtful vanity, by which the people of
each country are apt to prefer themſelves
to thoſe of every other; and to make their
own cuſtoms and manners and opinions
the ſtandards of right and wrong, of true
and falſe. The ſame propenſity, ſays another author †, is the moſt remarkable in
the whole deſcription of mankind.

* Letters on the Study of Hiſtory, p. 29.
† Hiſtory of Civil Society, p. 145.

National

National vanity is indeed confined to no æra in civil life. If the epithets *Greek* and *Barbarian* are oppofed to each other in the *Greek* tongue, epithets, exactly equivalent, are oppofed to each other in an *Indian* tongue, fpoken on the coaft of Labrador; and, in general, the names by which the rude American tribes wifh to be diftinguifhed, are affumed from an idea of their own pre-eminence *. If the learned Chinefe were mortified with the figure their empire made in the general map of the world, the poor natives of Congo pronounce themfelves highly favoured among mortals: and the moft wretched of African tribes folace themfelves, under all their misfortunes, with the fond perfuafion that, whitherfoever they go, they fhall, one day, return, in life or in death, to their native fhores.

* Hiftory of America, vol. i. p. 412.

Such

Such partiality, when not carried into an extreme, anfwers a noble end : and the pureft patriotifm is often founded on local circumftances, and a predilection for eftablifhed forms. But that preference of affection to our own country, which is the true definition of patriotifm, is compatible, furely, with fuitable regard and allowances for the various afpects of humanity.

Profound ignorance, and a contrariety, or repugnancy of cuftoms and manners, account for that averfion, or contempt for ftrangers and foreigners, implied in the partial fentiments of favage and untutored tribes. No information, no experience, no conviction can always conquer early prejudice : and the Hottentot, who returned from Europe, relapfed, we may believe, with all imaginable eafe, perhaps with additional fatisfaction, into the eftablifhed habits of his country.

But

But fuch examples are balanced by others of an oppofite nature, no lefs remarkable, which hiftory prefents to our view: examples of docility, of emulation, of magnanimous preference. Some of thefe it will be proper to recite, if we would not belie the character of the ruder ages.

The Romans, while yet a rude people, difdained not to appoint an embaffy to enquire into the jurifprudence of the Greeks, and to fupply, from that fountain, the deficiencies in their civil code.

This embaffy feems to have been fuggefted by Hermodorus, an exiled citizen of Ephefus, who afterwards eminently affifted in interpreting the collection of laws brought from Greece. His public fervices met with a public reward. A ftatue was erected to him in the Comitia at the public expence: an honour which the jealoufy of Rome would have denied to a ftranger in a lefs generous age. But, at this period, fhe acted from a nobler impulfe; and the ftatue erected to Hermodorus was erected, in reality, to her own honour. Yet the name of this Ephefian, which cafts a luftre upon Rome, feemed to caft a fhade upon his native city; and that people, according to Heraclitus, deferved to have been extirpated, to a man, who had condemned fuch a citizen to exile [C].

The Romans, in other inftances, were capable of acting with the fame humble dignity.

They difdained not to refer to the court of Areopagus at Athens, the decifion of fuch queftions as were too complex or intricate for their own tribunals. This reference, that embaffy, may feem worthy of a people who were deftined, one day, to be the rulers of mankind. But the policy of rude nations, though feldom called into

view

view unlefs by that fortune which renders their pofterity illuftrious, is often, we may believe, conducted with the fame fpirit.

In the reign of Hadrian, and Antoninus Pius, references, from the fierceft barbarians, to Rome, were not uncommon. And there occurs an example of policy, in modern ages, lefs celebrated indeed, but more liberal, perhaps, and magnanimous than any recorded in Roman annals. It relates to religion, an object certainly the moft fublime and interefting that can enter into public councils and deliberations.

A duke of Ruffia, while his fubjects were yet pagans, fent abroad commiffioners to inform themfelves, on the fpot, concerning the religion of Rome, the religion of the Greek church, and the religion of Mahomet, that he might determine, upon the report of thefe commiffioners, which of thefe feveral religions it became him to

M 2 embrace

embrace and eftablifh, as the guardian of
his people. So much modefty in acknowledging domeftic infufficiency; fo much
candour in weighing the pretenfions of
foreign inftitutions, are rarely to be met
with in the proceedings of nations reputed
civilized. And if we compare the fentiments which thófe under a different ftate
of the arts are difpofed to entertain, we
fhall find that undiftinguifhing contempt,
though mutual in fome refpects, fubfifts
between them by no means in an equal
degree. It is commonly mitigated, on the
one fide, by credulity and admiration, to
which the ruder nations are peculiarly
prone [D]; while it is heightened, on the
other, by antipathies, which the pageantry
of rank, and the exterior of polifhed life,
are apt to infpire.

The congrefs of mankind, at Conftan-
tinople, during the period of the crufades,
opened perhaps a fairer field for this comparifon,

parifon, than any other occurrence in the annals of the world. Various people in different ftages of civil culture, convened, as it were, at a general rendezvous, and paffing in review before each other, muft have impreffed the mind with emotions and fentiments correfponding to the variety of their conditions. Hiftorians, fpectators of the fcene, and animated with the paffions of their contemporaries, have defcribed the impreffion of this fingular interview; and from the defcriptions of thefe hiftorians we may collect the judgment of nations.

The Greeks exulting in their unrivalled fuperiority in arts, looked down on all the ftrangers affembled in their capital, with fupercilious contempt, and, on fome, even with deteftation. The Latins, on the other hand, and in general the ruder ftrangers of the Weft, with more modeft ideas of their own accomplifhments, reccgnized a degree of refinement in manners and in arts, fo

M 3   far

far superior to their own, and regarded
with an admiration approaching to enthufiafm, the fplendor and magnificence of the
Greek empire.

The leaders of the crufades, accordingly,
on their return from the Holy Land, abandoned in fome fort the rufticity of their
manners, and aimed at fome reformation
in the tafte and fciences of Europe. And
to thefe wild expeditions, fays an admired
hiftorian*, the effect of fuperftition or folly,
we owe the firft gleams of light, which
tended to difpel barbarity and ignorance.

In general it may be affirmed, that rude
nations are touched with fome degree
of reverence or admiration at the fight
of dignified appearances; that they honour, at fome diftance, that ftate of the
arts towards which they are tending; and
that it is only in cafes where the diftance
is too immenfe for their profpect or

* Hiftory of Charles V. vol. i.

conception,

conception, that they acquiefce in their condition with an apparent infenfibility, and allow their fuperiors to poffefs unenvied greatnefs.

The Saracens, notwithftanding the defolation of literature at Alexandria, which marked their firft conquefts, foon appeared in the fcene, as its moft zealous champions. Eager to preferve, as before active to deftroy, they cultivated its precious remains with unexampled ardour. A novelty was even to appear in public negociations: a people contending for erudition as for empire, and actually demanding the works of the antients, by exprefs articles, in treaties with the Greek emperors [E].

Modefty is confiftent with the moft afpiring views. It is the actual poffeffion of refinement and civil arts, not the efforts made towards acquiring them, which engenders extravagance and conceit. A few

M 4　　　　frivolous,

frivolous, or at beſt ornamental diſtinctions, are miſtaken for real differences: and if we ſurvey the circle of human things, the illuſions of vanity, and the inſolence of pride, will be found moſt inherent to nations and to ages intoxicated with proſperity and affluence.

Commerce, the boaſt of modern policy, by enlarging the ſphere of obſervation and experience, promiſed to undeceive the world, and to diffuſe more liberal and equal ſentiments through the ſeveral parts of an extended ſyſtem. But commerce, it is to be feared, has, in ſome inſtances, been productive of the very contrary effects; and by expoſing, if I may ſay ſo, the nakedneſs of ſociety, and uniting, in one proſpect, its moſt diſtant extremes, has heightened the inſolence of nations, and rendered their original and natural equality, to a ſuperfi‑cial obſerver, more incredible.

In

In judging of nations, as well as of individuals, our obfervations are more frequently directed to circumftances of pomp and outward fplendor, than to intrinfic excellence. And countries, accordingly, where no fuch appearances are to be found, we too haftily conclude to be the manfions of people, who, from a natural inferiority of talent, are incapable of producing them.

This conclufion was drawn firft by the Egyptians, and afterwards by the Greeks. The Greeks, more efpecially, regarded their own country as the feat of every perfection; and policy, and refinement, and arts, as their exclufive privilege.

Extravagant as the opinion now appears, it was the opinion of free and of polifhed ftates, in the meridian of their courfe. It was fupported by a comparifon with the neighbouring nations; nor then, perhaps, directly

directly contradicted or difproved by any authentic memorials.

Such prefumption, therefore, was more excufable in the antients; but having been, long fince, reprobated by the fulleft experience, ought to afford a leffon of wifdom and moderation to all fucceeding ages.

When it is obferved that, in proportion to the age of the world, the known regions of civility are of larger extent; it is not being too fanguine to expect, that, in the lapfe of time, the whole habitable globe fhall be found compatible with the fame improvements.

What avails it that experience refutes fo amply the errors of paft times, if it corrects not our judgment of the future, nor difengages the mind from the dominion of its former prejudices ?

3 Could

Could the perpetual greatnefs of one people be fet in oppofition to the perpetual meannefs of another, the plea of natural pre-eminence were exceedingly fpecious. But it is great conjunctures only which form great men ; and there are certain periods in the annals of the moft diftinguifhed nations, wherein they appear in no degree fuperior to their contemporaries.

In that long interval, which elapfed from the age of Alexander to the conqueft of Greece by the Romans, there is fcarcely an Athenian of eminence upon record. And the obfervation, with a few exceptions, is applicable, perhaps, to the whole of Greece, from the above age as far down as the Achæan league, when Agis, and Cleomenes of Sparta, and Aratus, and Philopæmen give us fome idea of their illuftrious anceftors.

When

When we revolve, therefore, the rife and decline of nations, and the fluctuating character of the fame people at different æras, we muft neceffarily allow to mankind, in thofe countries at leaft which have been the principal fcene of civil hiftory, an equal rank and importance in the fcale of being.

Let us then examine the plea of humble and unafpiring nations, not hitherto fuppofed to have emerged into diftinction, or to have touched the neareft verge of fcience and the liberal arts. Conftituted fo long in circumftances fo far beneath the ftandard of our ideas, it may be deemed not unreafonable to impute to *them* an original inferiority of nature, or a degradation of rank, occafioned by the infallible operation of phyfical laws.

Were the facts fully afcertained, and otherwife inexplicable, fuch conclufion might be embraced and warranted upon the

the principles of found philofophy. But the facts are deftitute of evidence; and, even if we admitted their reality, none of thefe hypothefes would be neceffary to folve the hiftory of the world.

Let us carry our imagination back to an æra more antient than the birth of arts. Let us then fuppofe an obferver, of profound difcernment, to predict, from a feries of calculation, the eventual fortune of the world, exclufively of all regard to foil or climate, or at leaft to the fuppofed influence of the heavens on the human mind. His fagacity, perhaps, might not determine where civil arts fhould firft arife, or fhine forth with the fulleft luftre: yet far, furely, from expecting them, in all countries, to be coincident in their origin, or to flourifh, at once, in the fame degree, he would expect confiderable intervals between the arrival of different people at points of equal advancement.

4   So

So various are the causes which concur to the full establishment of regular and well-constituted government; that no evidence decisive of the relative capacity of any people could be derived from the commencement of their civil æra. Even after the first movements have been successfully made, there are a thousand disasters, which may annoy a political constitution, in its infancy or early youth, and not suffer its principles to ripen into perfection. Circumstances in no degree affecting the genius of a people, are often sufficient to circumscribe their progress; and consistently with the full strength and vigour of the human powers, the reign of ignorance and simplicity may endure for ages.

Although great attainments indeed imply great talents, the want of talent is not implied in disappointment. In the researches, for instance, of science and philosophy, lofophy, the moderns have not only equalled, but furpaffed the antients: yet who, upon this foundation, will arraign the genius of antiquity?

Fortune governs events : and the magnitude of genius or capacity, in individuals or in tribes, cannot be fully eftimated by the fuccefs of its exertions. Even the actual promoters of the moft important interefts of mankind have feldom anticipated, in idea, the progreffive confequences of their own plans. In eftimating human attainments, their origin, progrefs, and perfection, muft not be totally afcribed to human wifdom. And, with all due honour to the memory of our forefathers, this judgment may be pronounced on all the arts, fciences, and governments they have delivered down to pofterity ;

—— Quod divum promittere nemo Auderet, volvenda dies en attulit ultro!

But,

But, if the approaches to civility are eafily made, whence then, it may be afked, have we fo many embarraffing theories concerning the origin of language, the rife of political union, and the effential arrangements of focial life? While fuch proceedings, in the judgment of the learned, feem to exhauft all human wifdom and ingenuity, is it not, in reality, more wonderful to find fo many nations already emerged from obfcurity, within the compafs of a few thoufand years, than to find fo many others ftill hovering on the confines of a ftate of nature?

But, in farther illuftration of this point, let us indulge a few arbitrary fuppofitions.

Let us fuppofe the number of men, born with the high prerogative of conducting a people eventually within the line of civilized life, is to the reft of the fpecies in a certain fixed proportion.

Let

Let the chance of such men being placed in circumstances favourable to the enterprize, form another proportion. And in circumstances thus favourable, let the chance against disappointment by natural or violent death, or other contingency, form likewise an element in the problem. Then, by compounding these proportions, it follows that one only, out of a determinate number of men, is born to execute this great design.

Now let us imagine the earth already peopled before civilization began, and that the number upon earth, at any one time, is equal or inferior to the number which results from the above proportions; then, judging from the probability of things, one or more generations must pass away, after the earth is fully peopled, before civilization is any where introduced. And, after its introduction into any one corner, the numbers in the uncivilized part of the

N earth,

earth, being then lefs than the whole fpecies, ftill more generations, commencing
from the former æra; muft pafs away,
before the æra of civility to any other
people.

In proportion therefore to the nations
already emerged, the chance for the emerging of any new people muft conftantly
decreafe.

The computation indeed fuppofes no
intercourfe between the civilized and the
barbarous nations. By reafon of that intercourfe the chance of extending civility
rifes, no doubt, in an eminent degree.
Hence, with regard to countries poffeffing
intercourfe, the progrefs may be exceedingly
rapid. But in the other, and fequeftered
corners of the globe; calculation determines
that there is a growing chance againft the
appearance of a cultivated or polifhed
nation. And, if we reafon from actual
expe-

experience, it is far more probable that, in any barbarous land, the civil arts will owe their original to foreign operations, either hoftile or commercial, than to interior efforts.

The Romans were no lefs the legiflators, than the conquerors of the world. While fpreading defolation with their arms, and trampling on the liberties of mankind, they were actually anticipating, in every country, the progrefs of legiflation, and the arts of government: and the fame people, in their fall, left to their barbarous conquerors the traces of a jurifprudence, to which Europe was principally indebted for its future progrefs.

Nor are we to regard the Romans as inventors of arts, or as the founders of their own policy. The elements of both were drawn from a foreign fource. Even the Greeks, in forming their plans, copied

N 2   more

more diſtant originals. Pythagoras and Plato, Lycurgus and Solon, had read the Pillars of Egypt: and the maxims of the Greeks were drawn from the philoſophy, if not from the legiſlation, of the Eaſt.

Similar obſervations are applicable to all the freer ſtates: and if, according to Mr. Hume, pure deſpotiſm, once eſtabliſhed, cannot poſſibly, by its own native force and energy, refine and poliſh itſelf, and re-publican and free governments are the only proper nurſery of arts and ſciences, we have hence an additional principle to account for their late appearance or ſtag-nation in ſo many parts of the earth. Perhaps then, ſince the world began, there are a few only, perhaps but a ſingle people, who owe their riſe and illuſtration to bold and original efforts of the human mind.

If therefore a concurrence of ſuch va-rious cauſes is found requiſite, if not to produce,

produce, at leaft to accelerate the progrefs of refinement and arts; that progrefs muft be proportionably retarded by a different contexture of events. But the habitations of barbarifm, at any one period, muft in fpeculation appear immenfe, when we farther reflect, that the tranfition from barbarifm to civility is not more incident to mankind than the contrary tranfition [*F*].

How many nations have *certainly* fallen from that importance, which they had formerly borne among the focieties of mankind, let the annals of the world declare! How many more have *probably* experienced as fatal a reverfe, we affume not the province of determining. But revolutions, to us unknown, various nations may have undergone; while, being expofed to our view only in their decline, a judgment has been formed of their general character, from what is peculiar to a certain age.

N 3

In

In examining into the antient ftate of a country, our opinions may be guided by tradition, or by hiftory, by the genius of language, or of arts, or by the declaration of external monuments. In dubious cafes rational conjecture may reft on one of thefe modes of evidence, or may be balanced nicely on them all.

Let us imagine a modern traveller to perform the tour of the Eaft. He finds there a country, under the gloom of barbarifm, prefenting no traces of erudition or civil arts, and without all tradition or memorial of anceftors fuperior to the rude inhabitants. Yet hiftory might inform him, that the natives of this country had once been as confpicuous and flourifhing, as their pofterity are now obfcure. Such perhaps is the condition of Babylon, once the wonder of the world. Such is the condition of the antient Colchis, which once, if we believe the writings of Pliny or

of

of Strabo, abounded in riches and in people, and formed the centre of a great commercial fyftem.

Let us next imagine our traveller to arrive in a land as barbaroufly peopled, and unmentioned, or undefcribed, in the writings of any hiftorian. There however, we will fuppofe, are preferved fome monuments of art and grandeur, far difproportioned to the general afpect of things, and to the actual pofture of affairs. Might he not hence diftinguifh a ftate of depreffion from a ftate of nature, and the laft from the firft movements of civil fociety?

Nor is the fuppofition purely imaginary. Within the prefent century, difcoveries have been made in the wilds of Tartary, which feem to declare that country to have been the manfion of a great people; or, at leaft, to indicate a fall from fome of

N 4   the

the more elevated forms of fociety. The fcene of thefe difcoveries, lying between Siberia and the Cafpian Sea, is now filled with a nation of Calmucs fubject to the Ruffian empire: and on fuch evidence the Czar Peter founded his opinion, that the arts had made the tour of the globe [G].

On principles exactly fimilar, more recent difcoveries ferve to confirm the large advances of the antient Etrurians, in elegant and polite attainments, before the fettlement of any Grecian colony within the limits of Italy.

Nor are fuch indications confined to any latitude or climate.

The country of Cambodia *, in the torrid zone, uncultivated as the natives now are, prefents appearances to the traveller, which, unfupported by hiftory or tradition,

* Les Voyages d'un Philofophe, par M de Poivre, p. 102.

6   may

may be regarded as memorials of former greatnefs.

Even in the new continent, though, in all probability, more recently peopled than the old, there are indications of a fimilar import.

The account, publifhed by Mr. Kalm, of an expedition acrofs North America, contains fome curious information. The expedition was undertaken by a French party from Canada, under the protection of the French government. After traverfing immenfe deferts, a country of a more promifing appearance, retaining veftiges of agriculture and civil life, opened to their view. Amidft the wildnefs of nature, they perceived an artificial face, and recognized the relics of a former age [*H*].

The teftimony of other travellers is no lefs decifive. On the fhores of the Miffifippi,

fippi, and in other parts of the new continent, there have been found works of
great antiquity, which evidence an acquaintance with military fcience, far above
the capacity of rude and untutored tribes *.

Well then may it be inferred, that there
are large chafms in the annals of many
countries; and that we have obtained but
an imperfect acquaintance with the fortune
of governments, and the viciffitudes of the
fpecies.

There are certain correfponding points in
the rife and decline of nations, which are
liable to be confounded. And apparent motion may be as different from the real, in
the political as in the natural world.

Unacquainted therefore as we are with
the ftated returns of the civil period, we
may miftake the evening for the morning

* See Carver's Travels through North America.

I   twilight;

twilight; and imagine a people to be juft emerging from the fhade, who have, long before, paffed their meridian, and are haftening back within the limit of darknefs.

The clear teftimony of profane hiftory reaches no higher than the Greeks and Romans. There is no piercing through the gloom of remoter ages. And even the contemporary fituation of other governments is faintly defcribed, or mifreprefented, or paffed over in contemptuous filence.

Such facts as the above, it is not pretended, can fupply the defect. They may rectify fome errors; they may fhed fome feeble rays of light on nations of dubious exiftence, but cannot redeem their memory from oblivion. They furnifh however new matter to the antiquarian, and a new topic in the circle of the learned.

They

They do more. They ferve to vindicate the prerogatives of the fpecies, and to fuggeft confiderations of fome weight in the deductions of philofophy.

Other fources of information unopened by the Greeks remain ftill to be explored. The *grand annals of China*, the books of the Bramins, and other immenfe collections of Oriental records, may form a valuable fupplement to the general hiftory of the world. Yet, amidft the darknefs and uncertainty in which hiftory and chronology are involved, it appears that the wide differences which have fubfifted, or fubfift at prefent, in the actual condition of tribes and nations, are fuch as, without prejudice to our nature, and exclufive of the unequal influence of the heavens, might, in part, be apprehended from the nice contexture of events, and the complicated operation of moral caufes.

But

But if the honours of nations were, in reality, to be eftimated by riches, by population, by the antiquity of arts, or by the ftability and duration of civil government, it is not any of the European nations, it is the Chinefe, and the Indians, who muft be placed at the head of the fpecies.

Let the lovers of paradox* contend that thefe antient people are merely the depofitaries of fciences delivered to them, in greater perfection, by a people who flourifhed in the North of Afia, but have long fince difappeared in the political fcene.

Let others contend that China was colonized by Egypt, and inherited the fciences from the parent ftate, who diffufed them over the eaftern as over the weftern world. Fix their original manfion in the high latitude of Siberia, or in the torrid zone, it is certain that they devolved on the Chi-

* L'Hiftoire de Aftronomie ancienne, par M. Bailly.

nefe

nese and the Indians in an early age; and
the uninterrupted poffeffion of fo noble an
inheritance is their diftinguifhing privilege.

But the confequences of this privilege
are, it muft be owned, of an ambiguous nature. And, if the criterion of civility has
been rightly defined *, many an obfcure
people have poffeffed it in a degree of perfection which the proudeft nations in Afia,
or in Europe, could not boaft in the days
of their fplendor.

If the picture of manners delineated in a
performance, which is now read and admired in almoft all the languages of Europe,
is a faithful copy of an original, it is no
paradox to affirm, that the court of Fingal
was as highly civilized as the court of
Lewis XIV.

* Effay IV.

In

In the one the arts were totally unknown; in the other they were at the height of their splendor. But the want of those graces which the arts confer, was more than compensated at the one court, by virtues in which the other was deficient. And if fidelity, generosity, true dignity of mind, are preferable to difingenuity, perfidy, servile adulation; if the former qualities are to be numbered among polite accomplishments, and the latter to be placed in the opposite column, who would not prefer the civilization of Fingal's court to that of the other, though embellished by all arts and sciences [I]?

Without presuming then to decide the dubious pretensions of mankind, it is our design, in prosecuting these general views, to enquire in what manner the progress of society is connected with local circumstances which do not immediately affect genius, or capacity. And from hence a

more

more accurate judgment will be formed concerning their direct and original influence on the human species.

Such discussion will lead us to enquire how far local circumstances, which, in a variety of ways, may prove beneficial or malignant, are rendered subject to our dominion and controul. And, having thus contemplated man as, in some sort, the arbiter of his own fortune, a question will arise, no less curious than important, whether the perfections and imperfections of his character in one age, may not act, with a direct influence, on the original fabric of posterity.

This is the field of speculation, which, in the order here stated, it is proposed to touch in the following pages.

NOTES.

N O T E S.

Note [*A*], p. 155.

LIVY, in the perfon of a Roman Conful, has defcribed in ftrong colours the degeneracy of the antient Gauls fettled in Afia, and of the Macedonians difperfed over various climates of the world.

Galli, fays he, jam degeneres funt; mixti et Gallogræci verè, quod appellantur. Sicut in frugibus pecudibufque, non tantum femina ad fervandam indolem valent, quantum terræ proprietas cælique, fub quo aluntur, mutat. Macedones, qui Alexandriam in Ægypto, qui Seleuciam ac Babyloniam, quique alias fparfas per orbem terrarum colonias habent, in Syros, Parthos, Ægyptios degenerârunt.

Liv. lib. 38. cap. 17.

Thefe are perhaps the exaggerations of Roman eloquence. But if the degeneracy exifted in

O the

the full extent of the defcription, it may probably be afcribed not more to phyfical than to
moral caufes : and it is not climate, but rather
a communication of manners that affimilates
the different races of mankind.

If the antient Gauls, who emigrated into
Afia, enervated by the reigning manners of
Bithynia, degenerated, according to Livy, from
the character of their hardy anceftors ; the modern French, who have occupied the Ifle of
Bourbon for a full century, are defcribed, by a
well-informed writer, as equal to the moft athle-
tic of the European nations.

Orm's Military Tranfactions, vol. i. p. 95.

Note [B], p. 156.

THIS memorable edict was iffued by Paul
the Third, in the year 1537. But, if the
doctrine of fome late publications had made its
appearance in the fixteenth century, it might
have fuperfeded the neceffity of this edict, by
fhewing that Ourang-outangs are, in reality, the
aborigines of all nations.

Such is the *illuftrious* pedigree of mankind!

NOTE

Note [C], p. 162.

ALTHOUGH there is no mention of Hermodorus in Livy, it is clear, from the teftimony of other writers, that this citizen of Ephefus was very inftrumental in directing the attention of the Romans to the Grecian jurifprudence.

Whatever relates to this celebrated embaffy is an object of learned curiofity. The felection therefore of a few paffages from antient authors, tending to authenticate the particulars mentioned in the text, may not prove unacceptable to fome of my readers.

The pretenfions of Hermodorus are acknowledged, in the Pandects of Juftinian, in the following paffage:

Alias duas ad eafdem tabulas adjecerunt: Et ita ex accidentia appellatæ funt leges duodecim tabularum: quarum ferendarum auctorem fuiffe Decemviris *Hermodorum* quemdam Ephefium exulantem in Italia quidam retulerunt.

Digeft. lib. 1. tit. 2. fect. 4.

The erection of the ftatue is mentioned by Pliny:

O 2

Fuit

Fuit et Hermodori Ephefii in comitio legum quas Decemviri fcribebant, interpretis, publici dicata (viz. ftatua).

Plin. Nat. Hift. lib. 34. cap. 11.

Cicero quotes Heraclitus thus:

Eft apud Heraclitum phyficum de principe Ephefiorum Hermodoro; univerfos ait Ephefios effe morte multandos, quod, cum civitate expellerent Hermodorum, ita locuti funt: Nemo de nobis unus excellat: fin quis extiterit, alio in loco et apud alios fit.

Tufc. Difput. lib. 5. cap. 36.

The fame quotation from Heraclitus I find in Strabo, lib. 14. with only this difference, that the Ephefians *under age* are not involved in the condemnation.

The fame anecdote is likewife related by Diogenes Laertius, in the Life of Heraclitus.

NOTE [D], p. 164.

IN ages of ignorance and fimplicity, mankind are fo prone to credulity and admiration; that thefe propenfities, prior to reafoning, feem to lead favages into the acknowledgment and adoration of invifible powers, and to introduce,

in

in every country, the rude elements of popular fuperftition.

From hence, therefore, a cultivated people derives an importance, which has often been abufed, though fo capable of being directed to the beft interefts of fociety.

The natives of the Weft Indies regarded Columbus and his companions as fuperior beings, fprung from heaven, who had defcended to vifit the earth, and were worthy of divine honours.

———Nova progenies cœlo dimittitur alto.

How honourable then would it have been for the European nations, had they extended their authority in the new hemifphere by perfuafion, not by arms, and had a reverence for their religion, their virtue, and fuperior wifdom, conducted them to empire.

Note [E], p. 167.

THERE is but one occurrence in the hiftory of public negotiations, more fplendid than this conduct of the Saracens; the conduct of that king of Syracufe, who made it an exprefs condition in a treaty with the Carthaginians,

nians, that they fhould abftain from human
facrifices.

It is noble in a people to demand fcience
from their enemies. It is nobler to demand of
enemies not to be to themfelves inhuman.

NOTE [*F*], p. 181.

OUR phyfical and moral fyftems, fays a
writer whofe eloquence is not always fufficient to fupport his philofophy, are carried
round, in one perpetual revolution, from generation to corruption, and from corruption to
generation; from ignorance to knowledge, and
from knowledge to ignorance; from barbarity
to civility, and from civility to barbarity. Arts
and fciences grow up, flourifh, decay, die, and
return again, under the fame or other forms,
after periods which appear long to us, however
fhort they may be, compared with the immenfe
duration of the fyftems of created being. Thefe
periods are fo difproportionate to all human
means of preferving the memory of things, that,
when the fame things return, we take frequently for a new difcovery, the revival of an
art or fcience long before known.

Bolingbroke's Phil. Works, vol. ii. p. 224.

The

The moderns, however, may frequently be confidered as original in difcoveries and inventions anticipated by the genius of a former age.

The true folar fyftem was taught probably by Pythagoras, above two thoufand years ago; yet Copernicus was not indebted for his knowledge of it to the Pythagorean fchools. Nor would it neceffarily derogate from the merit of modern difcoveries, fhould we admit a propofition maintained in a late performance, which abounds in curious erudition, *Qu'il n'eft prefque pas une des decouvertes attribuées aux modernes, qui n'ait eté, nonfeulement connue, mais même appuyée par de folides raifonnemens des anciens.*

Recherches par M. Dutens.

It is well obferved by a writer, who illuftrates the nature of genius with the happy precifion of a philofopher, that more of it is often exerted in perfecting an art than in the firft invention. On this account he ranks the Greeks above the Egyptians in the fcale of genius; and feems to queftion the frequency of its appearance among the Chinefe, who have not hitherto been able to

advance

advance the arts beyond that mediocrity to which they had attained in ages the moſt remote.

See Dr. Gerard's Eſſay on Genius, p. 19 and 25.

NOTE [G], p. 184.

MR. VOLTAIRE, in his deſcription of the country of the Calmucs, gives the following account of theſe diſcoveries. C'eſt-là qu'on a trouvé en 1720, une maiſon ſouteraine de pierres, des urnes, des lampes, des pendans d'oreilles, une ſtatue equeſtre d'un prince Oriental portant un diademe ſur ſa tête, deux femmes aſſiſes ſur des trônes, un rouleau de manuſcrits, envoyé par Pierre le Grand à l'Academie des Inſcriptions de Paris, et reconnu pour être en langue du Tibet : tous temoignages ſinguliers que les arts ont habité ce pays aujourd'hui barbare, et preuves ſubſiſtantes de ce qu'a dit Pierre le Grand plus d'une fois, que les arts avoient fait le tour du monde.

Hiſt. de l'Empire du Ruſſie, tom. i.

The ſubterraneous houſe mentioned in this paſſage by Mr. Voltaire, is deſcribed more particularly,

ticularly, by our Englifh traveller Mr. Bell, as a regular edifice, fituated in the midft of a defert, on the banks of the river Irtifh, and diftinguifhed by the name of the *Seven Palaces.*

According to the tradition of fome Tartars, it was built by Tamerlane the Great: according to that of others, by Gengifchan. But certain countries of Tartary, of a more northern fitua-tion, which, according to Mr. Bell's informa-tion, the arms of Tamerlane had in vain at-tempted to fubdue, appear to have been once the fcene of great tranfactions; and contain the fpoils of nations of high antiquity, and no ftrangers to the arts.

Some Calmuc manufcripts were purchafed by Mr. Bell at Tobolfky ; and, having been prefented by him to Sir Hans Sloan, are now depofited in the Britifh Mufeum.

See Bell's Travels, vol. i. p. 209.

There is another fpecies of evidence, which, in the opinion of fome writers, is ftill more conclufive.

The

The exiſtence of a great nation in the north of Aſia, long before the dates of our moſt antient memorials, has been lately contended for, on aſtronomical principles, by M. Bailli, a writer of great learning and ingenuity. He contends, that the original ſeat of mankind was ſituated in the high latitude of 49° or 50°; that the primitive migrations were from North to South; and that we find in the Eaſt the fragments only of ſciences which were carried thither by the primitive emigrants, but which were never generally known to the Indians or other Orientals.

I cannot attempt in a note to examine the foundations of this theory. It is ſufficient to obſerve, that it has not as yet been able to ſhake the eſtabliſhed conviction of the learned.

M. Bailli, in a ſeries of letters addreſſed to the late M. Voltaire, labours to convert that author to his opinions; and from a ſympathy, no doubt, which reigns among congenial ſpirits, he eſpouſes an hypotheſis of Monſ. Buffon, concerning the earth and the whole planetary ſyſtem, ſtill more fanciful than his own concerning

cerning the origin of nations, and the progrefs of arts and fciences.

Note [H], p. 185.

THESE intelligent travellers, having fo-journed in the country for fome time, had an opportunity of examining it with attention.

The country is fituated at the diftance of nine hundred French miles weft of Montreal. And, befides other monuments of antient cultivation, there were found in it pillars of ftone, of great magnificence, manifeftly erected by human hands, but of which there remained no tradition among the Indian tribes. Unfortunately, thefe pillars contained no infcriptions, whence any conjecture could be formed concerning their original. At length, however, a large ftone, in the form of a pillar, was difcovered, and fixed in it a fmaller ftone covered with unknown characters. This ftone, fevered from the larger mafs, being carried to Canada, and from thence to France, was delivered into the cuftody of M. Maurepas, at that time fecretary of ftate.

Note

NOTE [*I*], p. 191.

A WELL known writer in politics affects to have ideas of the ſtate of mankind ſo *mathematically* preciſe, that he divides the Indians of America into three claſſes, *mere ſavages, half-ſavages*, and *almoſt civilized*.

The ſavages he deſcribes, in all reſpects, as a blood-thirſty, unfeeling race, deſtitute of every human virtue. But miracles have not yet ceaſed. The miſſionaries of Paraguay, we are told, can transform theſe infernal ſavages into the moſt benevolent race under heaven. A metamorphoſis which, though celebrated by a dignitary of the church, will hardly command belief in this ſceptical age : yet it ſerves to ſupport a new theory of government, which is founded on the total debaſement of human nature, and is now oppoſed to a theory that aſſerts its honours, and derives from a happier origin the image of a free people.

See a work by Dean Tucker, Part II. containing, as the writer *modeſtly* declares, the true baſis of civil government, in oppoſition to the ſyſtem of Mr. Locke and his followers.

When

When the benevolence of this writer is exalted into charity, when the fpirit of his religion
corrects the rancour of his philofophy, he will
learn a little more reverence for the fyftem to
which he belongs, and acknowledge, in the
moft untutored tribes, fome glimmerings of
humanity, and fome decifive indications of a
moral nature.

E S S A Y VI.

OF THE GENERAL INFLUENCE OF CLIMATE UPON NATIONAL OBJECTS.

THE influence of climate on the policy, if not on the character of nations, is acknowledged by every obferver of human affairs.

To eftimate this influence, in the various regions of the globe, were an arduous problem. But, by attending to the diftinct modes of its operation, we may be able, perhaps, to fet bounds to its empire.

Climate then may be regarded either as a natural principle, acting with powerful energy, or with irrefiftible impulfe, on the

fabric

fabric of our being; or it may be regarded merely as a local circumſtance leading to a variety of action in the œconomy of civil life. Viewed in this ſecondary light alone, it will appear eminently to affect the progreſs of arts and government.

The means of ſubſiſtence, the ſubject of art, the incitements to induſtry, the ſcene of its operations, ſo diverſified in the ſeveral diſtricts of the earth, muſt affect proportionably the courſe of affairs. And in circumſtances ſo diſſimilar, it would be ſtrange, if the conduct of the actors were governed preciſely by the ſame laws, or every where attended with the ſame ſucceſs.

The genius of mankind, far from being equal, muſt have been as various as the ſituations in which they are placed, did we obſerve all nations exalted to an equal pitch

pitch of civility, or of eminence in arts and sciences.

To a peculiarity of situation, and often to the urgency of occasions, nations as well as individuals owe their greatness. Pressed with no difficulties, and not conscious of wants, mankind in general love repose. The calls must be loud and frequent, which animate their exertions, and urge them forward in active or laborious pursuits.

In countries therefore of original affluence, supplying spontaneously, or with little culture, the necessaries of life; arts will remain long neglected, or will be cultivated slowly, and with inferior ardour. But in countries, more penurious by nature, the deficiency is supplied by the resources of industry and invention.

In the former situation the genius of mankind lies dormant, or is feebly exer-

P   cised,

cifed, or evaporates upon fubjects which make but little figure in the hiftory of civil fociety: Of confequence, many characteriftics of primitive fimplicity will be long preferved: and a people may increafe and flourifh, to a high degree, before they have recourfe to the partition of land, the divifion of labour, and the diftinctions of private property; circumftances which firft open domeftic commerce, diverfify and embellifh the ranks of life, and furnifh out the objects of a regular œconomy.

Unacquainted with thefe objects, men foothed by indolence, or immerfed in the gratifications of fenfe, are furely in no condition to eftablifh a plan of government upon rational or juft foundations. Yet the habits formed among them, in the infancy of fociety, gradually break the mind for political fervitude. The defire of equality is balanced by a regard to exterior accommodations; and the love of fafety,

of

of pleafure; or of eafe, triumphs, in every competition, over the paffions which are the natural guardians of law and liberty.

Such, in fome climates of the world, is the real defcription of mankind. Habits chiefly incident to polifhed ages, vitiate and enfeeble the favage life. And the ufual *effects* of refined and commercial arts in the decline of civilized government, are *caufes*, in thefe climates, which, operating from the beginning, fuperfede their origin, or obftruct their growth.

To be unaffifted then by arts, yet obnoxious to the evils with which they are commonly affociated, is, confidered in a moral or in a political light, one of the hardeft difpenfations of fortune.

In other countries, the imbecility of government derives often a temporary fupport from the very arts which tend to

P 2   its

its deſtruction. Thus the commercial opulence of Carthage prolonged her exiſtence for half a century, by ſatiating the avarice of Rome. Thus Rome herſelf, when no longer able to defend her empire by arms, was able by ſubſidies to poſtpone her fate.

Rome indeed, in her better days, could reſiſt the moſt deſperate onſets of barbarians: for to equal enthuſiaſm in arms, ſhe added ſuperior ſkill in the art of war. When the Cimbri and Teutones, in the career of glory and of victory, were preparing to croſs the Alps, Marius, by one deciſive blow, cruſhed that formidable invaſion. Yet the deſtroyers of the Roman name were one day to come from the ſame quarter. The nations of Scythia, ſituate between the Euxine and Caſpian ſeas, having been exterminated by Pompey, directed their courſe, under the conduct of Odin, towards the north and weſt of Europe. They eſtabliſhed themſelves in the almoſt evacuated

evacuated fettlements of the Cimbri and Teutones, where incorporating with the feeble remnant of the fpecies, they repaired the ftrength and population of the North. And it was their defcendants, now confounded with the northern nations, who, returning fome ages after, retaliated on the Romans the calamities inflicted on their forefathers, and on mankind.

A people, however, fo long progreffive as the Romans, could fall only by degrees. The refources of the Roman government were not exhaufted with Roman virtue.

The Goths, who, by the memorable defeat of the Emperor Decius, had become mafters of the Illyrian provinces, were induced by the pecuniary conceffions of the fucceeding emperors, to abandon their conquefts. Conceffions fo pufillanimous, I am not ignorant, have been fup·pofed to haften the fall of Rome: but they

P 3   feem,

seem, at this conjuncture, to have been as
neceffary as they were inglorious, and the
feeble expedients of a declining empire in
the crifis of its fate.

A variety of fuch expedients, in calamitous periods, policy and arts afford. But
the communities of mankind, in the climates above defcribed, by a cruel fatality,
are deftitute of the ordinary refources of
government, whether in a rude or cultivated age.

Their peculiar circumftances, then, with
regard to foreign powers deferve attention.
The fame original and luxuriant profu-
fion which fo long exempts them from
labour, and difpenfes with arts, and poft-
pones the affignation of property, expofes
them the more to the envy and hoftile
defigns of other ftates. In proportion to
the fertility of their fettlement, the poffeffion of it is the more precarious. To defend

fend that settlement, is almoft the fole end of public union: nor will the apprehenfion of danger from abroad allow their attention to fix upon the objects of interior government. Implicit fubmiffion to the command of a fuperior, an idea fo requifite in the conduct of armies, and in the fcience of war, infinuates itfelf into the frame of their political conftitution. In fupporting political exiftence, they part with all the ideas of natural liberty: and the rigour of defpotifm alone, controuling the tendency of their manners, can fecure that command of the national force which, in times of public danger, is neceffary for the protection of their country. To avoid therefore the condition of a conquered people, they acquiefce in a conftitutional tyranny, perhaps not lefs oppreffive.

Thus danger from abroad concurs with their domeftic circumftances in the fubverfion of their natural rights; and neither the ope-

rations

rations of peace nor of war supply the occasions which animate a rising people.

The spirit of liberty, in its full strength,
is not always superior to the sense of public
danger.

When thirty cities of Latium, confede-
rated with the Sabines, threatened to crush
in its infancy the Roman commonwealth,
consternation and terror seized all ranks of
men. And the dictatorship, a sort of temporary despotism, and a solecism in a free
government, owed its original establishment to this alarming conjuncture. The
confederacy, however, was quickly dissolved: the battle at the lake Regillus was of a
decisive nature; and the men who had ex-
pelled the Tarquins were able to rule the
storm. But had such perils, which were
transient and accidental, been inherent in
the soil; had the Romans been more liable
to suffer, than prone to commence hostili-
ties;

ties; had the poffeffion of a more productive or extenfive fettlement drawn upon
them at firft the envy of mankind, inftead of
animating their own ambition, the neceffity
of public affairs muft have foon rendered
that magiftracy perpetual, which was at
firft of fo limited a duration, reforted to
only in great emergencies, and during the
flourifhing ages of the commonwealth altogether difcontinued.

Let us imagine, then, the fpirit of liberty
already languifhing, menaced with danger
like that which made the Romans tremble,
but arifing from fixed and permanent
caufes, and we imagine the circumftances
of mankind, in climates which eftablifh
and perpetuate a defpotifm more abfolute,
more formidable, and more degrading,
than the dictatorfhip of Rome [A].

A nation determined by external fituation to embark in fchemes of dominion,
poffeffes

poffeffes immenfe advantages in war over any other nation who arms merely for defence. The principles of intereft, of ambition, of glory, embolden the defigns of the former, and give to their efforts irrefiftible impetuofity. The efforts of the latter are more conftrained and reluctant; and the moft profperous fuccefs ultimately terminating in a temporary fecurity rather than in pofitive acquifitions, produces not the martial ardour and enthufiafm which actuate heroic minds.

Hence the formidable incurfions of the antient Scythians, and the unequal oppofition of the Afiatic ftates. Hence the difficulties encountered by the Romans in extending their conquefts in Europe, and their more eafy triumphs on the theatre of Afia. Hence we may obferve, on the one hand, the aftonifhing career of the northern conquerors, who overturned all the governments of Europe, and on the other, the

feeble

feeble refiftance made to their progrefs by more opulent and luxurious nations.

The Spartans are almoft the only inftance of a warlike people who, by fyftem, abftained from conqueft. Yet was it confonant with the maxims of Spartan policy to transfer every war to a diftance from the feat of government. And during a period of fix hundred years, which elapfed from the firft eftablifhment of the Dorians in Lacedæmon to the reign of Agefilaus, no foreign enemy had dared to fet foot in Laconia. To render that country the theatre of war, was referved for Epaminondas.

" Many of you," faid an Argive to a Spartan, " fleep on the plains of Argos."—" Not one of you," replied the Spartan, " fleeps on the plains of Lacedæmon."

Sparta,

Sparta, though great in war, was fingu-
larly formed for peace, for virtue, and for
harmony. The rigour of domeftic difcipline rendered war a relaxation from toil.
And the duration of its civil government
was owing, in a great degree, to the confinement of territory, to the love of juftice,
to the exclufion of luxury, of money, of
commerce, and of arts and fciences.

There is a nation too, defcribed by Tacitus, who feem to have been diftinguifhed
among the antient Germans, as the Spartans were diftinguifhed among the antient
Greeks; and though their territory was
more extenfive, to have refembled the
Spartans in the maxims of their policy,
and in fome features of their national character [B]. But though fuch examples of
wifdom and moderation fometimes occur,
and adorn hiftorical annals, the rules of
diftributive juftice are commonly little re-

garded

garded by nations in the career of military glory.

The nature of climates, the comparative fertility of countries, by determining the courfe of offenfive war, and by affecting the meafure of fubordination in civil fo-ciety, muft be allowed no inconfiderable fway over the general fortune of the world: and circumftances apparently the moft favourable prove often, in their con-fequences, the moft adverfe to the great proceedings of nations.

Nature, in fome climates, like an over-indulgent parent, enervates the genius of her children, by gratifying at once their moft extravagant demands. In other cli-mates fhe difpenfes her bounty with a more frugal hand, and, by impofing harder conditions, impels them to induftry, trains them up to enterprize, and inftructs them

in

in the advantages of arts and regular government.

But the extremes of munificence and rigour, by withholding the motives to induſtry, or by rendering the ends defperate, often produce fimilar effects. A middle fituation between thofe extremes is perhaps the moſt eligible in a moral light, as well as the moſt aufpicious for civil progrefs.

Mankind, however, in the various climates where they have fixed their habitations, will long preferve a genius and character wonderfully correfponding with the various difcipline of nature. One people, enured to difficulties, become addicted to hardy enterprize. Another people, bleffed with eafe, exert their talents in refined fpeculation, rather than in active purfuits.

The fpeculative fciences accordingly can be traced back to infancy in Chaldæa, in
India,

India, in Egypt, and countries that verge to the torrid zone; while we obferve them attain to full growth and perfection only in the higher latitudes.

In thefe latitudes their connexion with arts is recognized, their importance to fociety more fteadily kept in view, and a rank and eftimation affigned them, regulated in part by that ftandard. But in thofe lower latitudes, cultivated from other confiderations, they retain long their primeval form, and with little reference to mechanical or vulgar arts, command, on their own account alone, the veneration of the people. Yet rendered fubfervient perhaps to the ends of fuperftition, or an engine of defpotic power, they may have contributed more to fink and debafe, than to improve and dignify the fpecies.

Religious fentiments and opinions, which are coëval with the beginnings of refinement,

ment, and which, when duly regulated, are fo beneficial and ornamental to fociety, may thus, by falfe affociations, affume a form, and inftil paffions which difgrace reafon and humanity. Accordingly in the countries firft enlightened by fcience, the religious paffions have ever fermented with the greateft violence, and produced the moft aftonifhing effects.

Under their impreffion, a wild race from Arabia proved an overmatch for valiant and hardy nations. For, by this fpirit, the Saracens arofe; and turning the tide of conqueft, which had run fo generally from north to fouth, into an almoft oppofite direction, threatened, by the progrefs of their arms, to reverfe the hiftory of the world [C].

In the fame climates have reigned, at different periods, the moft abject fuperftition, the wildeft fanaticifm, the moft fublime

lime theology: and, exclufive of the pure and divine inftitutions of the true religion, many of the rites and obfervances propagated over various and diftant regions have originally centered there.

But to account for fo ftriking an effect in any latitude or climate, there is no need to recur to the pofitive and direct influence of the outward elements on the human mind. The feries of events, once begun, is governed more perhaps by moral than by phyfical caufes: and this propenfity of genius and temper may owe its original to the primary direction of the fciences, and their early alliance with theology and civil government.

The fciences corrupted in their fource, or perverted in their application, were early inftrumental, among the nations of the Eaft, in confecrating abfurdity, and giving confiftency to error. Dreffed up in the folemn airs of myftery, they abetted

Q   religious

religious impofture; and ferved, in the hands of priefts and civil rulers, as a charm to allure and fafcinate the crowd. Augury, divination, and fuch wretched literature as tended rather to corrupt than toim–prove the underftanding, were, above all other learning, admired and cultivated. The motions of the heavens were ftudied, in order to difcover the imaginary influences of ftars: and a, fcience which opens the nobleft view of the univerfe, and is fo capable of being directed to valuable ends in civil life, was connected in its origin with the credulity and fuperftition of mankind.

In Chaldæa, the moft antient feat of aftronomical obfervation and difcovery, judicial aftrology was held in fupreme and univerfal efteem. Pythagoras, the moft accomplifhed mafter that ever flourifhed in Greece or Italy, borrowed his ideas from the Magi of Chaldæa, from the Gymnofophifts of India, or from Egyptian priefts, was admitted into their colleges, initiated into

into the myfteries of their religion, and by *them* inftructed in the true fyftem of the world.

But the myfterious fciences of Pytha-goras were foon forgotten in the Italic fchool. The Romans occupied, from the inftitution of their commonwealth, in fcenes of action, had no tafte or leifure for fuch purfuits. With invincible prejudices againft the Chaldæans, and other Orientals, and with no turn towards aftrology, they regarded their character and erudition with equal and undiftinguifhing contempt. From the reign of Numa there had elapfed a period of above five hundred years, when Julius Cæfar, aided by the fuperior learning of the Eaft, adjufted the civil year, with fome accuracy, to the true annual period, and eftablifhed, on aftronomical principles, the reformation of the Roman calendar.

Yet the Romans as far excelled thofe other nations of antiquity in the fabric of

their

their jurifprudence, and in the application
of the true principles of government, as
they were excelled by them in aftronomy,
in geometry, in phyfics, in theological
refinements, and in all the abftract deductions of philofophy.

In general, fertile and luxuriant countries feem peculiarly fitted to be the
nurfery of refinement: becaufe leifure
awakens curiofity; and curiofity leads to
purfuits that fill up the vacancies in human
life. Every new fituation prefents to man
new objects of folicitude and care. The
demands of animal nature no longer bound
his defires. The fcene now opens to the
intellectual eye. He marks the relations,
and dependencies of things; and learns
to contemplate the world and himfelf.

Conftituted in fuch circumftances, what
more natural to a mind, fomewhat elevated
above common life, than this foliloquy:

" Where

" Where am I! Whence my original! What my deftiny!—Is all around me dif-cord, confufion, chaos! or is there not fome principle of union, confiftency, and order?—Am I accountable to any fuperior? connected with any great fyftem of being? ——Is this contracted fpan of life the whole of man? or was he born with higher expectations, and for nobler ends? Is there a power above to juftify that hope!"—

Various opinions will afterwards arife, in the courfe of philofophical generations, concerning the œconomy of invifible powers. Various rites will be inftituted to render the Divinity propitious, and, fince fear predominates in moft religions, more to avert his wrath. But thofe queftions are the fuggeftions of nature, and, in the more productive regions of Afia and Africa, gave a beginning to the philofophic age. Yet, in fuch regions,

Q 3 from

from the want of the chief incentives to action, the improvements of civil life will seldom arrive at a high pitch of eminence or perfection.

Countries of a different description will be flower in their first improvements; because an attention to the neceffary functions of life allows not fufficient leifure for obfervation, or the fublimer culture of the underftanding. But fciences and arts tranfplanted hither in a maturer form, take root and flourifh ; and alleviating the toils or enlarging the accommodations of fociety, grow up to an extraordinary height, gradually removing the obftacles which prevented their more early eftablifhment.

Here too the mechanical arts, which owe their maturity, if not their birth, to the more preffing occafions, or increafing demands of mankind, become fubfidiary to

the

the fublimer fciences, and advance them beyond the limit affigned them in their antient feats. To this fortunate alliance, the labours of the learned in modern Europe have been indebted for one half of their fuccefs: and, this alliance broken, the fciences, in our climates, would fink down to the level at which they have ftood fo long in the climates of Afia.

The genius of nations is more or lefs turned to peace or war, to fpeculation or action. The more fpeculative begin improvements; and the active conquer; yet improve often upon the improvements of the vanquifhed.

Thus the fituation of the fpecies in one country is more advantageous to the firft openings of refinement, from circumftances which allow a freedom to genius, and an exemption from animal toil: while their

Q 4   circum-

circumftances, in another country, con-
duce more effectually to the farther extenfion and cultivation of the liberal arts.
And thefe effects, frequently refulting
from foil and climate, whofe temper depends fo often upon the pofition of the
globe, mark a fundamental and fixed diftinction between the communities of mankind in the lower and higher latitudes.

The temperament indeed of countries is
diverfified by a variety of caufes, natural
and artificial, which we fhall not attempt
to enumerate. Elevation above the level
of the fea has fometimes a decifive influence, and confers many of the advantages
of the temperate zone on countries that
approach almoft to the equator. But notwithftanding a number of exceptions, the
more general character of climates correfponds with the aftronomical divifions of
the earth. And fuitably to this courfe of
                                    nature,

nature, the fame civil order of things, which we have remarked in the antient continent, feemed to have been preparing in the new.

The fun of fcience arofe there, as on our fide the globe, on the confines, or within the limit of the torrid zone. Civilization had begun, and even made fome progrefs, in the empires of Peru and Mexico, while mankind in all the upper latitudes were utter ftrangers to refinement, in the loweft ftage of political union, and, like the antient Germans, fcarce acquainted with fubordination in civil or domeftic government.

Their æra of civility has not yet arrived. The fyftem to which they belonged was unhinged by violence. But had the Peruvian and Mexican arts been tranfplanted into thofe regions of the new hemifphere, they would, in all probability, have flourifhed there, from the fame combination of

caufes

caufes as in Europe, with a degree of vigour and fuccefs unknown in the more productive and fertile climates which gave them birth.

The new world, from its connexion with the old, opens to the arts and fciences an oppofite career. And in contradiction to the firft arrangements, and the apparent order of phyfical laws, they will be carried by a more impetuous current, along the ftream of political events, from the northern to the fouthern climates.

It becomes not, perhaps, a Briton, a private citizen, at fuch a crifis, to anticipate this order of things; to predict the revolutions of government, or the eventual glory of a future age.

This chapter of accidents fhould be read in the cabinets of Europe.

It

It is local circumſtances alone whoſe tendency we are contemplating in both hemiſpheres: and to open the extent of that influence in the general ſyſtem, it is neceſſary, as in the following Eſſay, to deſcend into ſome farther detail.

NOTES.

N O T E S.

NOTE [*A*], p. 217.

I HAVE mentioned the office of Roman Dictator, as being the most extraordinary concession, which the exigency of public affairs ever extorted from a free people.

Had such an accumulated jurisdiction been transferred to one man, by a solemn act of the whole legislature, it might be vindicated, perhaps, on the principles of state necessity. But when the right of nomination was vested in a single consul, without the consent, against the will of the people; and without even a decree of the senate, though that sanction was indeed necessary to confirm the consul's nomination; we observe, with astonishment, among a people jealous of their rights, an engine of government one of the most tremendous, in appearance, that ever hung over the liberties of mankind.

It

It deferves however to be remembered, that the authority of Dictator, while it annihilated in a moment every other authority in the ftate, left the tribunitial power untouched, whofe influence formed a fort of conftitutional controul on the proceedings of that formidable magiftrate. Yet more admirable far is the policy of the Britifh government, in fuch extremities as called for a Dictator under the Roman.

In England, to borrow the language of a late noble author, well read in the conftitution of his country, " In England, where a mixed con-
" ftitution of government unites the powers of
" monarchy, ariftocracy, and democracy, much
" more happily than that of Rome ever did,
" even in its beft ftate, if extraordinary dangers
" require that the Habeas Corpus law (the
" great fecurity of our freedom) fhould for a
" time be fufpended, it can only be done by the
" joint advice and authority of the whole legif-
" lature. And if, in any cafe where delay
" would be fatal, the fafety of the public appa-
" rently obliges the king, in whom alone the
" executive power refides, to act againft this
" or any other law, without having been pre-
" vioufly impowered fo to do by both houfes
" of

" of parliament, his minifters are refponfible
" for it to their country, and can no otherwife
" be fecured than by a bill of indemnity, which,
" if the neceffity pleaded for their juftification
" is found to have been real, the Lords and
" Commons will not refufe to pafs. But, in
" Rome, a fingle conful, agreeing with the fe-
" nate to name a dictator, without the concur-
" rence, and againft the will of the people,
" might fubject, at any time, the liberty and the
" life of every Roman citizen to the arbitrary
" power of one man, fet above all the laws, and
" in no way refponfible, for the exercife of his
" fovereignty, to the juftice of the ftate. In-
" deed after the end of the fecond Punic war,
" the fenate itfelf grew fo jealous of the danger
" of this office, that, for an hundred and
" twenty years before Sylla took it up, no Dic-
" tator was appointed."

Lord Lyttelton's Works, p. 36.

In one inftance, perhaps the only one to be
met with in the Roman annals, the fenate referred the choice of a Dictator to the people;
and the Conful Marcellus named Quintus Ful-
vius in obedience to their order.

Liv. l. 27, c. 5.

Note

Note [B], p. 220.

THE Spartans are not degraded by a comparifon with this virtuous people, whofe
chara&ter is thus delineated by the Roman
hiftorian:

Tam immenfum terrarum fpatium non tenent
tantum *Chauci*, fed et implent: populus inter
Germanos nobiliffimus, quique magnitudinem
fuam malit juftitia tueri. Sine cupiditate,
fine impotentia, quieti fecretique, nulla provo-
cant bella, nullis raptibus aut latrociniis popu-
lantur. Idque præcipuum virtutis ac virium
argumentum eft, quod ut fuperiores agant, non
per injurias affequuntur. Prompta tamen om-
nibus arma, ac fi res pofcat, exercitus: pluri-
mum virorum equorumque: et quiefcentibus
eadem fama.

Tacit. de Morib. Germ. c. 35.

Note [C], p. 224.

HAD the Saracens, a&uated by the fame
fanatical fpirit, begun their career fome
centuries fooner, they might have met, with
equal force, the barbarians of the North, and
contended

contended with them for the fpoils of the weftern empire. Or perhaps the encounter of fuch armies might have prolonged its date.

When the Saracens, in the eighth century, after the conqueft of Africa, appeared in Spain, the Goths fettled there, degenerated from the valour of their anceftors, were in no condition to make head againft fuch invaders. The conteft would have been very differently maintained by thofe Goths, who, in the fifth century, paffed the Pyrenees, and bid defiance to the mafters of the world. But now the empire of the Caliphs was foon eftablifhed in Spain. And the Saracens, after the reduction of that country, meditated the conqueft of all Europe. They became mafters of that part of Languedoc which had been fubject to the Goths; and were marching on, in confidence and triumph, to complete their defigns, when fortunately for the Chriftian world, in the year 731, they were defeated in a pitched battle by Charles Martel, the champion of the faith, and the moft renowned general of the age.

To eftablifh the Mahometan religion all over the earth by the fword, was conformable with its avowed maxims. Predeftination too was an article

article of faith that ferved to heighten the conftitutional valour of the Saracens, which was ftill farther enflamed by an opinion inculcated by their leaders, that to die in battle fecured infallibly to every Muffulman an immediate entrance into paradife, and an introduction to the beatific vifion.

Their valour however had been fignalized before the age of Mahomet; and it is not pretended that religious enthufiafm acted alone, without the co-operation of other caufes, in the eftablifhment of the Moflem yoke.

" Pour expliquer, fays Montefquieu, cet evenement fameux de la conquête de tant de pays par les Arabes, il ne faut pas avoir recours au feul enthoufiafme. Les Sarrafins etoient, depuis long temps, diftingués parmi les auxiliaires des Romains, et des Perfes: les Ofroeniens; et eux etoient les meilleurs hommes de trait qu'il y eut au monde: Severe, Alexandre, et Maximin en avoient engagé à leur fervice autant qu'ils avoient pu, et s'en etoient fervis, avec un grand fuccès, contre les Germains, qu'ils defoloient de loin: fous Valens, les Goths ne pouvoient leur refifter; enfin, ils etoient, dans ces temps-la, la meilleure cavalerie du monde."

Grandeur et Decadence des Romains, ch. 22.

R

E S S A Y   VII.

BESIDES the comparative fertility of foils, the nature of their productions, and the pofition of the globe, there is a variety of local circumftances, which, by affecting the feries of public events, are intimately connected with the civil order of the world.

The divifion of a country by mountains, by lakes, or rivers, the vicinity or diftance of the fea, infular or continental fituation, and the relative condition of the furrounding nations, are caufes which affect, in an

R 2   eminent

eminent degree, the nature and fuccefs of public enterprize.

A fixed fettlement is, in the order of things, an indifpenfable preliminary to the improvements of civil life. Men unattached to any foil, but accuftomed to perpetual migration, are in no condition to cultivate arts, and feem incapable of conducting, for a length of time, any well-ordered fyftem of operations. Such loofe and disjointed members compofe no regular body. Individuals incorporated into no fteady form, nor kept together by any local ties, can maintain only a temporary and precarious union, and deferve not the name of a nation. The progrefs then of mankind in every climate is confiderably affected by the form and extent of their original fettlement. And the occupants of an immenfe tract of country, where nature has fet no bounds to difperfion, nor erected barriers againft the incurfions of other tribes,

feem

feem to be moft inaufpicioufly conftituted for the maintenance of civil liberty, or the growth of civil arts.

Unhappily, the genius of man, in the ruder ages, is peculiarly turned for war. The internal diffenfions among the fame people, or the hoftile defigns of different tribes, gave occafion, we may believe, to the firft arrangements of political fociety.

The ideas of property ripen by flow degrees; and the maxims of jurifprudence are regulated by the fortune of arms.

In a country, therefore, affording no re-treat to the vanquifhed, it is fcarce poffible, in the ruder ages, long to preferve the free-dom of mankind. And while fervitude is the only alternative compatible with fub-fiftence, in this extremity, the moft reluct-ant fpirits will finally bend under the yoke of dominion.

R 3   Such

Such caufes operating at firft within a
narrow fphere, will afterwards prevail
with a more diffufive influence. In proportion to the number of the vanquifhed
tribes, the fubjection of other tribes will
be accomplifhed with greater eafe: till at
length various and diftant nations, whofe
poffeffions were feparated only by imaginary lines, falling fucceffively under one
dominion, the manfion of a little commonwealth becomes the capital of a vaft empire.

Thus reluctant nations coalefce into a
fyftem. The fame caufes which proved
deftructive of their rights, in the firft
ftruggles of political life, will render future attempts for the recovery of them
extremely hazardous; and the enlargement of territory beyond the antient limit,
will more effectually prevent that union
and concert, in the operations of fubjects,
                                    which

which lead to the introduction of the more liberal plans of government.

The voice of liberty will be heard no more. She can no longer arm her affo-ciates in the caufe of humanity. The monarch of a great empire fits fecure upon the throne, and fets at defiance the mur-muring of the people and the revolt of provinces.

In this pofture of things, the reign of defpotifm may long endure. The rival-fhip and jealoufy, which animate independ-ent ftates, ceafe to animate this larger fyftem: nor can the fciences and arts which raife and adorn fociety, be prefumed to flourifh under the malignant influence of a conftitution tending fo manifeftly to the debafement of the human fpecies.

Such confequences then may be traced up to a geographical fource. Nor will the

R 4

evils

evils hence refulting, exhauft their force in
the open tracts of country where they began to flow. The torrent which covered
the plains rolls on, with increasing violence, and the beft fenced territories are no
longer able to refift its progrefs. Nations,
accordingly, fituated with many advantages
for interior policy, and whofe frontiers
feem little expofed to external annoyance,
may have thefe advantages more than balanced by a dangerous vicinity to a growing empire.

We obferve the nations of Tartary not
only deftitute of arts, but, notwithftanding
barrennefs of foil, and the poffeffion of a
climate accounted favourable to the independency of man, condemned to all the
rigour and tyranny of defpotic power [A].
A country, the nurfe of heroes, that has fo
often fent forth tribes to be the conquerors
of Afia, fees herfelf involved in the general
                                     fervitude;

fervitude; and an acceffion to empires fubdued by her own arms.

The Arabians perhaps are the only
people under heaven who have remained,
in all ages, exempt from a foreign yoke.
Confident againft the world on Arabian
ground, they refifted the fucceffive attempts
of the Affyrian, Perfian, Grecian, and Roman arms. Yet the vicinity of thefe empires was not regarded with indifference.
It filled them with continual alarms, it
circumfcribed their projects, confined their
genius to defenfive war, and retarded the
cultivation of the liberal arts. But when,
in the decline of the Roman power, other
nations prefumed to be ambitious, the
Arabians were capable of forming extenfive plans of military and civil enterprize.
Yet, in their own deferts alone, they are
invincible, and there the race of Ifhmael
maintain to this day an independence on
the Ottoman empire. There the human
mind

mind is ftill capable of bold and liberal efforts. A new fect of religion has, of late, appeared in thofe regions, of a genius uncommonly elevated*. It explodes every fpecies of idolatry. It 'enjoins the belief and worfhip of one eternal Being, the fovereign of the world, and eftablifhes the doctrines of pure theifm on the fole foundation of reafon and nature. It confiders Mofes and a number of his fucceffors in the Eaft, as fublime teachers of wifdom, and, as fuch, worthy of refpect and reverence. But it rejects all revelations, and denies that any book was ever penned by the angel Gabriel. How far this religion may diffufe itfelf is yet uncertain. But, though it may breathe a while in the free air of Arabia, it never can be cherifhed or tolerated in the Ottoman empire, where fuperftition is fo neceffary to conduct the machine of government.

* Defcription de l'Arabie, par M. Niebuhr.

Thus

Thus the fortune of the Arabians correfponds with the defcription of their country,
which fecures them from foreign conqueft,
and determines the meafure of their obedience
to civil power. And whether the hiftory of
this extraordinary people is accounted for
by natural caufes, or by a fpecial interpofition of Providence, the prediction concerning them is equally fulfilled: nor can it
derogate from the authority of holy writ,
that we obferve the determinations of heaven to coincide with a regular and eftablifhed order of fecond caufes.

But the connexion of a fettlement with
the more general fortune of mankind is
chiefly difcernible in the production of
extended government.

As the political divifions of territory,
though fluctuating and precarious, have,
however, at all times, fome neceffary dependence on the natural and permanent
divifions

divisions of the terraqueous globe, the
consequences arising from the magnitude
of states and empires may often be referred ultimately to a geographical source.
Local circumstances alone have set bounds to
the devastation of conquest, and to the rage
of war; have checked the tyranny of governments, and prevented the establishment
of an universal empire: an establishment of
such alarming tendency, that we can scarce
resist supposing it to have been one design
of Providence, in the natural divisions of
the earth, to supersede the possibility of an
event that would have proved so fatal to
the improvement and liberties of mankind.
Instead of those happy distinctions which
furnish incentives to genius; instead of
that variety of arts and sciences which owe
their existence to bold and original efforts
of divided nations, there must have subsisted, throughout the earth, an uniformity
of conduct and manners subversive of all
liberal enterprize.

The

The different ages of society, like the different ages of man, require different discipline and culture. The maxims of policy applicable to one part of the world, are not always applicable to another; nor are the full advantages of any local œconomy reconcileable, perhaps, with fubordination to a general fyftem. If therefore the beft inftituted government falls fhort of perfection, in order to improve its advantages it is neceffary to circumfcribe its dominion. To fix indeed mathematically the proportion of territory or of people, which is moft confiftent with public profperity, and with the benefits of civil life, is an impoffible problem in the fcience of government. But it is certain there are limits with regard to both; and all the inconveniencies of univerfal dominion will be felt, in an inferior degree, throughout an extended empire.

Public affairs there fink into a quiefcent form, genius is fettered by authority, or

borne

borne down by the weight of the prevailing fyftem.

In fmall ftates men of wifdom have
arifen, whofe credit with the community
has enabled them to patronize arts, and
to conduct plans of public utility to the
moft fuccefsful iffue. Legiflators and politi-
cians, acting at fome favourable crifis, have
been known, within a narrow circle, to
controul eftablifhed cuftoms and manners,
to reform civil inftitutions, and to innovate
in all the effentials of government. But
the reformation of a wide domain is an
immenfe and laborious work, that needs a
long preparation of time, and prefuppofes
an intercourfe with regions enlightened by
philofophy and learning.

The reformation by Peter the Great is
one of the moft memorable in the annals
of extended government. The flourifhing
condition of the arts in the fyftem of nations,

tions, with which he connected his empire, was peculiarly favourable to the grandeur of his views.

The Czar availed himself of the conjuncture. Like the founders of antient states, he travelled into foreign nations to study mechanical and commercial arts, and legiſlative wiſdom, and the whole ſcience of government. By inviting artiſts and manufacturers from thoſe nations to reſide in his empire, he tried, by their example, to allure his people into the occupations of civil life. To a profound diſcernment of his true intereſts, and to conſummate ſagacity in forming commercial and civil plans, he added all the qualifications moſt conducive to their ſucceſs. Boldneſs, vigour, perſeverance, he poſſeſſed in an eminent degree. And the example of a ſovereign, who was himſelf a proficient in the detail of the arts, muſt have produced a wonderful effect on a people over whom

3   his

his authority was unlimited. The eftablifhment too of a ftanding army, which
confirmed that authority, and carried his
commands with irrefiftible force through
the remoteft provinces, tended to ftrengthen
and maintain all his other eftablifhments.
And at laft his triumphs in arms, which,
at the treaty of Newftadt, rendered him
the arbiter of the North, and fecured the
tranquillity of his empire, favoured all the
plans of his interior policy.

Yet fo glorious a reign could animate a
few parts only, without infufing life or
vigour into fo vaft a body. The maxims
of his policy have been purfued with ability by fome of his fucceffors on the throne
of the Ruffias; and, above all, the prefent
Emprefs, by the protection of arts, by the
eftablifhments of her police, and by a well-
digefted code of internal laws, emulates
the honours of her illuftrious predeceffor;
perhaps,

perhaps, in some instances, eclipses his fame. But it is the misfortune of Catharine, as of Peter, to execute plans on too large a scale: and, with so rare advantages, it is by the courtesy of Europe, if the Russians, at this day, are permitted to rank among civilized nations. The limits of the empire must be contracted, to give rapidity to its movements. And the late accession of territory, how greatly soever it may augment the revenue, or the splendor of the sovereign, tends in reality to encumber, in those regions, the efforts of the human species. So repugnant is the genius of extended government to refinement and liberal arts.

The history of the Chinese alone seems to form an exception to the general theory. And it must be owned, that if a few nations have touched a higher stage of civility and refinement than that people, there

is

is none on the records of the world, who have enjoyed, for so extended a period, along with a large proportion of public felicity, a mediocrity in arts and sciences.

Yet if the sciences in that empire are not on the decline, they seem for ages to have been stationary, or slowly progreffive, and certainly have not arrived at such maturity and perfection as might be expected from the length of their courfe. Authority is there decifive of public opinion, and abridges the liberty of private judgment. Error is confecrated by antiquity. No spirit of philofophical enquiry animates the learned; and the freer excurfions of genius are unknown.

In antient times, when the Greater and the Leffer Afia was divided among a number of states; when Affyria, Phœnicia, and Egypt, formed independent governments, science feems to have dawned upon the world

world with confiderable luftre. But thefe
appearances gradually vanifhed. The firft
empire of the Affyrians was not aufpicious
to mankind. Their fecond empire, by the
union of Niniveh and Babylon, was ftill
more alarming. Yet the Affyrians, the
Medes, and the Egyptians, maintained a
fort of balance of power, and feem to have
flourifhed as rival and contending nations.
But no fooner the Perfians arofe, and the
world beheld at Perfepolis a government
more oppreffive, more formidable, and more
extended than had ever been erected at
Niniveh, or at Babylon, than human nature was degraded in the Eaft. And during a period of above two hundred years,
while all things went forward in the Weft
in little ftates, all things went backward
throughout the immenfe provinces under
the Perfian fway.

Prior to this revolution, our acquaintance
indeed with hiftorical annals is imperfect.

It

It is impoffible to defcend into the detail of
more antient government. Yet, on autho-
rities facred and profane, it may be affirmed, that, long before the Perfian greatnefs,
the Egyptians, and other Eaftern nations,
were in poffeffion of ufeful and ingenious
arts, and not unacquainted with maxims
of policy conducive to public felicity and
order.

Egypt was divided early into diftinct
kingdoms; and the dynafties which fill
her annals confifted, it is probable, of contemporary, not of fucceffive monarchs.
The reigns of her kings, before Sefoftris,
are celebrated as the reigns of the gods:
and, if any credit is due to the hiftory of
that conqueror, it was perhaps the power
of his arms which fhook the foundations
of antient governments, and brought on
the firft general cataftrophe of nations.

If

If however the empire of Sefoftris, like that of Alexander, devolved not entire upon his fucceffors, human affairs might have returned into their former courfe; or at leaft fome nations might have recovered their antient freedom and profperity.

What may have happened in a period fo remote, cannot now be determined with certainty. But, in periods well illuftrated, great monarchies arofe in the Eaft: and the continent of Afia, fo rarely interfected by mountains or rivers, feems to be the natural feat of extended dominion.

While European governments fo often fluctuate, enlarge or contract their limits, are torn afunder by inteftine commotions, or are overwhelmed with foreign irruptions, the great contefts for dominion on the theatre of Afia have feldom diverfified the form of Afiatic eftablifhments. General revolutions by conqueft, more fre-

S 3   quent

quent in that quarter than in Europe, have not been productive of similar effects. The Asiatic governments are soon re-established nearly on the same foundations; and one spirit predominates amidst all the viciffitudes of power.

The stability of the Chinese government, amidst the shocks and revolutions of conquest, is commonly alleged as a proof of the wisdom with which it is framed. But in a country of such extent and population, the disproportion of numbers between the conquerors and the vanquished, and the character of those conquerors who have no fixed usages, manners, or institutions of their own to come into competition with the established system, sufficiently account for its immutability, without regard to the degree of its perfection. And if the system of manners, laws, and religion, established in China, is not shaken or subverted by internal causes, it promises to withstand the

most

moſt furious inundations of the Tartars, and may go down triumphant to the lateſt poſterity. Thus China forms an illuſtrious example of the connexion of human affairs with geographical limits. Secure on the eaſt and ſouth by the ocean, and on the weſt by inacceſſible deſerts, ſhe is vulnerable on the ſide of Tartary alone. All her military operations are exhauſted in one direction, and with one view. And by the efforts of an induſtrious and active policy, ſhe erected, many ages ago, an artificial barrier for defence, unequalled for extent or magnificence in any other age or country. But that barrier, the work of men, could not defeat the intention of nature; and in defiance of their wall, it was neceſſary for the Chineſe to ſubmit to conquerors, who ſhould incorporate with them into one body, ſubject to the ſame head.

S 4   Next

Next in magnificence to that of China, is the wall of Caucafus, called by the Orientals the wall of Gog and Magog. It extended from the Cafpian to the Black Sea, and is fuppofed by fome antiquarians to have been built by Alexander the Great, in order to cover the frontiers of his empire from the incurfions of the Scythians. But it is probably a more antient fabric. The lofty fpirit of Alexander would hardly have ftooped to fuch daftardly policy; nor does it appear from the courfe of Alexander's victories, that he ever approached the Cafpian gates.

Such ftupendous monuments of art declare the fenfe of Afia concerning the magnitude of impending dangers; and equally indicate talents for pacific enterprize, and an incapacity for war. Yet if Afia were divided and fubdivided like Europe, climate alone would not give rife to

and

and perpetuate fuch general fervitude. And
if the defcription of Europe refembled that
of Afia, our climates would not be productive of freedom. The extended government of the Romans came to be as
violent and tyrannical as Eaftern defpotifm.
To maintain, therefore, a due balance of
power, and to prevent the rapacity of fovereigns from tranfgreffing thofe geographical limits which nature feems to have
affixed to dominion, is an object of the
firft importance to the general liberties of
Europe.

It ought alfo to be remembered by fovereigns grafping at dominion, that if, by the
connivance or fupinenefs of other powers,
they are fuffered to attain the ends of their
ambition, they affume a dangerous pre-
eminence; they exchange for precarious
greatnefs, the moft folid advantages, and,
by the magnitude of dominion, in a coun-

try

try like Europe, are likely to precipitate
its fall. Let them remember the counfel
of Auguftus Cæfar to his fucceffors, " never
" to enlarge the territories of the Ro-
" mans;" and learn, from the example of
that great people, to avoid the paths
which lead firft indeed to the fubverfion of
civil liberty, but finally to the diffolution
of empire.

The difcovery of America has opened
an immenfe field to the ambition of the
ftates of Europe. Inftead of augmenting
their territorial poffeffions at home, they
began, from that æra, to form diftant eftablifhments by conqueft or by colonization,
and to erect, in another hemifphere, a new
fpecies of empire. But between countries
fo widely feparated, a political union fubfifts with difficulty: and when difcontents
arife, diftance from the feat of government
affords

affords fingular advantages to provinces that meditate revolt.

Local preference can never be rendered confiftent with the beft ends of government. The relation of a colony to the antient country, rightly underftood, is a relation of perfect equality. The terms which denote parental and filial relation, when defcriptive of local ties, and intended to diftinguifh the cultivators of the antient foil from the cultivators of territory more recently acquired, are metaphors extremely liable to abufe. The one country is no more the mother, than it is the daughter. They are both the children of the fame political parent, and that parent is the government to which they owe equal allegiance.

But, when colonies are regarded in the light of fubordinate provinces, as appendages to government, and not entitled to

the

the same privileges and immunities with the parent-state, the lovers of civil liberty will acquiesce with reluctance in such invidious distinctions. Jealousies ripen into disaffection. Political independency figures in the imagination, and is aspired after as an elevation of rank.

The fabric of *colonial* subordination in all the governments of Europe seems to stand in need of repair. And unhappily, the freest of those governments was the first to be made sensible of its defects [*B*].

When the passions of a divided public were wound up to the highest pitch, when the charges of injustice, oppression, tyranny on one side, were retorted on the other by those of sedition, ingratitude, rebellion, argument and sound reasoning were little regarded in the contest. And at the instant when the wisdom of the British councils resolved, by the fullest communication

cation of privilege, and the moſt liberal conſtruction of provincial claims, to re-move every ground of jealouſy and diſtruſt, the inſidious interpoſition of a common enemy defeated the generous plan.

The Rubicon was already paſſed; and the colonies had dared to commit their cauſe to the events of war.

Perhaps there is room to hope that a ſenſe of common intereſt may ſtill prevail; that mutual affection and regard may again revive in people of the ſame manners, the ſame religion, and the ſame blood; and that ſome medium may yet be found to disjoin the American councils and arms from thoſe of France, and re-unite them, by more natural and indiſſoluble ties, to the Britiſh monarchy. To the ſtate of pu-pillage and dependence, which ſeems in-deed to be at an end, may ſucceed a con-nexion of a more equal and dignified nature,

nature, favourable to the happinefs and grandeur of both countries, and in which both countries may acquiefce with honour. But if mutual attachment fail, to recal American allegiance by the power of our arms, if not an impracticable, is certainly a moft hazardous attempt. It is to contend, in fome degree, with that courfe of nature, which fo often emancipates colonies at the age of manhood, and with all thofe local circumftances which threaten the difruption of empire.

The geographical divifions of the American continent are certainly aufpicious to civil liberty; and feem to oppofe the eftablifhment of fuch extended governments as have proved, in the antient hemifphere, a fource of the moft deftructive and debafing fervitude.

The local circumftances under review, whofe operations, in fo many inftances, are fully

fully difcernible, folve, we may believe, in
part, the hiftories of other countries, where
appearances are more equivocal ; and aided
or oppofed by other caufes, have been and
will be attended with confequences proportionably ferious and important all over the
globe. By their immediate connexion
with interior policy, they are, to a ftate
confidered apart from every other, of no
fmall account. But in the mutual relations of a number of ftates, the territory of
each, and the nature of its frontiers, by
affecting political independency and the
balance of power, prefent confiderations of
ftill fuperior moment.

To ftand fequeftered and alone is as fatal to
the genius of governments as to that of men;
and the nobleft enterprizes of art, or exertions
of policy, may often be referred to fituations
which have excited the rivalfhip, the jealoufy, and even the antipathy of nations.
Happy, in this refpect, were the govern-

ments

ments of antient Greece. Happy, on a larger scale, the governments of modern Europe. Posterity may perhaps contemplate the blessings of an equal and liberal intercourse, more widely disseminated. They may contemplate, from a concurrence of various causes and events, some of which are hastening into light, the greater part or even the whole habitable globe, divided among nations free and independent in all the interior functions of government, forming one political and commercial system. Or, perhaps, while every people is capable of progress, there is an incompatibility in the contemporary civilization of different regions: nor ought we to expect that perfection, which seems to be denied to every work of man, in the regulations of commerce, in the science of politics, or in the arts of civil government.

But

But I launch not on the immenſe ocean of poſſibility, and of future contingency. To compare paſt events, to eſtimate the actual attainments of men, and to point out their connexion with mechanical and local cauſes, is my immediate province.

T   NOTES.

NOTES.

Note [*A*], p. 248.

THE political fervitude of the Tartars is thus accounted for in the theory of Montefquieu.

In Afia there is properly no temperate zone. Without that gradation in the races of mankind which obtains in Europe, the ftrong nations are immediately oppofed to the weak. The Tartars accordingly make conquefts in the fouth of Afia, the region of pure defpotifm. But the defpotifm, congenial with thofe climates, is embraced by the conquerors, and fixing its roots in a great empire, extends its branches in all directions, till they finally overfhadow the plains of Tartary, and ftretch a far way to the North. Thus the part of Tartary, which bred the conquerors of China, is now annexed to the Chinefe empire. And even among the independent tribes, defpotifm, by the contagion of example, is equally predominant.

In

In parts of Tartary, colonized by the Chinese, the people are become mortal enemies to the parent ſtate; yet transferring to their new manſions the ſervile ſpirit of the Chineſe government, they remain, under a ſeparate eſtabliſhment, ſubject to deſpotic ſway.

L'Eſprit des Loix, l. 17, ch. 5.

NOTE [B], p. 268.

MR. HUME, in the firſt volume of his Eſſays, delivers an obſervation which ought, he contends, to be fixed as an univerſal axiom in politics, " that though free govern- " ments have been commonly the moſt happy " for thoſe who partake of their freedom; yet " are they the moſt ruinous and oppreſſive to " their provinces." But the maxim, though plauſible in theory, and illuſtrated by the examples of Rome and Carthage, ought not to be eſtabliſhed without limitation and reſerve.

The ſyſtem of colonizing among the Greeks was the moſt ſplendid that can well be imagined. Their colonies were conſidered from the beginning, as riſing ſtates flouriſhing under the guardianſhip and patronage of the antient governments; and were ſuffered, without jea-

T 2   louſy

loufy or diftruft, to rife to equal eminence and
diftinction. On the moft amicable and generous footing, an intercourfe was long maintained between the colony and the antient
government, tending to their mutual profperity.

But as a colony, thus eftablifhed, evidences
rather a generous dereliction of fovereignty in
the parent ftate, than the moderate exercife of
its dominion, the example of the Greeks will
hardly be confidered as forming an exception
from the above maxim concerning the peculiar
feverity of provincial government, as exercifed
by free ftates. Yet, if we pafs from antient to
modern times, it may be affirmed that, before
the date of the prefent conteft, the conduct of
the Englifh towards colonies, was lefs exception-
able than that of any other European ftate.
Spain and Portugal, not content with the advantages of an exclufive commerce, derive a direct
revenue from their American fettlements : and
the firft attempt of England to imitate the example of thofe imperious and arbitrary ftates,
created difcontents which were the immediate
fore-runners of revolt. Though the government of Spain had fcarce any merit either in
projecting, or in effectuating fettlements upon
the

the continent of America, the jealoufy of that government with regard to thofe fettlements knew no bounds. Of late, indeed, a more enlightened policy in the court of Madrid has fomewhat relaxed the rigour of oppreffion. England treated its colonies for a long time with neglect, and urged the higheft pretenfions to dominion, at that period when they were the moft capable of refiftance.

That provincial government, as it has been generally conducted, has been a fyftem of preference or reftraint, is confonant to the experience of ages. And the author of *Obfervations on the Nature and Value of Civil Liberty*, has rightly numbered all fuch governments among thofe which deferve to be accounted tyrannical and oppreffive. England can only claim the equivocal praife of being lefs tyrannical and oppreffive than the reft of Europe.

" In what way, then," fays a writer of found political difcernment, " has the policy of " Europe contributed to the firft eftablifhment, " or to the prefent grandeur of the colonies of " America? In one way, and in one way only, " it has contributed a good deal. *Magna virûm* " *Mater!* It bred and formed the men who

" were

" were capable of achieving such great actions,
" and of laying the foundation of so great an
" empire ; and there is no other quarter of the
" world of which the policy is capable of
" forming, or has ever actually and in fact
" formed such men. The colonies owe to the
" policy of Europe the education and great
" views of their active and enterprizing
" founders; and some of the greatest and most
" important of them owe to it scarce any thing
" else."

Dr. Smith's Enquiry, &c. vol. ii. p. 189;

ESSAY VIII.

THE SAME SUBJECT CONTINUED.

THE fate of nations often depends on circumftances apparently the moft trivial. The genius, the life, perhaps the temporary humour of a fingle man may, on fome occafions, fix the political arrangements that affect the effential intereſts of one half of the globe.

Local circumftances are fo blended in their operations with a variety of other caufes, that it is difficult to define them with fuch precifion as were neceffary to form an eftimate of their comparative importance. Hence the confufion, on this

T 4

fub-subject, which fills the volumes of the learned. A writer * of the first rank, who illustrates and adorns the history of mankind with plausible and ingenious theory, has assigned to *physical* causes an almost unlimited empire. Another writer †, no less illustrious, contracts into a point the sphere of their dominion. Their priority in the order of things, and their supposed permanency, have been urged by other writers, as decisive of superior sway. But it deserves to be remembered, that causes *physical* in their nature, are often *moral* only in their operations ; that these operations are limited and precarious, and relative to the conjuncture ; that a people may be long incapable to avail themselves of external advantages, that circumstances ultimately beneficial, may have proved for a long while incommodious or destructive; and,

---

* Montesquieu.   † Hume.

conso-

confequently, that the importance of local
ftation, far from being permanent, varies
not only with the contingencies of the
natural world, but with the courfe of political events, and the general ftate of human
improvement.

A fettlement conducing, at one period, to
render the natives fierce, treacherous, and
inhofpitable, may be inftrumental at another period, in rendering them civil and
humane.

Before the æra of navigation, a fettlement on an ifland, or the command of an
extenfive and commodious coaft, might
have conferred no advantages on the poffeffors; or rather circumftances, of fuch in-
eftimable account in a commercial age,
might, by cutting off all communication
with the reft of the fpecies, have proved,
in every former æra, invincible obftacles to

the

the civil arts. Our infular fituation, fo
fertile a fource of national fecurity, opulence, and grandeur, rendered us long an
uncultivated and fequeftered people:

——Penitus toto divifos orbe Britannos.

And the neglect with which Britons were
once treated in the fociety of nations, is
compenfated only by that attention which
their pofterity command. While nations
on the continent of Europe maintain their
barriers with difficulty, and at an enormous
expence, and, if they will confult their
fecurity, muft often court alliances, and
obferve, with jealous attention, the minuteft
variations in the balance of power, Great
Britain is exempted from fuch anxious
folicitude. By collecting her forces within herfelf, by avoiding continental wars,
which exhauft, to little purpofe, her treafure and her blood, and by rendering the
improvement of her maritime ftrength, the

4

fixed

fixed and steady object of her policy, she
may maintain, in defiance of powerful
confederacies, that post of honour and diftinction, which feems to have drawn upon
her the envy of nations, who now take
advantage of internal calamities to insult
her fortune.

The æra of navigation opened a new
species of correspondence among men;
and, in the infancy of the art, a civil settlement might be attended with peculiar advantages, which there could be no poffibility of tranfmitting, in their full extent, to
future generations. In the territory of the
Phœnicians, neither large nor fertile, yet
lying along a commodious coaft, we obferve fources of opulence and renown.
That country, oppreffed at firft by the
violence of the Affyrians, but afterwards
fo well adapted to the commercial circumftances of the antient world, called forth
in its people correfponding exertions, and
both

both invited them to undertake, and favoured the execution of early enterprizes
as a maritime power. While the Egyptians, in the fullnefs of riches and of pride,
and in the fpirit of an unfocial form of
fuperftition, had fhut their ports againft
mankind, and renounced all foreign correfpondence; it was the glory of the Phœnicians to venture beyond the boundaries
of antient navigation, and, by commercial
enterprize, to diffufe arts and civility over
the weftern regions. Bred up in habits of
frugality and domeftic induftry, the confequence of fcanty and penurious poffeffions, they purfued an œconomical, not a
luxurious commerce. The commodities of
every country were embarked on Phœni-
cian bottoms; and as merchants, or factors,
or navigators, they created a fort of univerfal dependence, and conducted, almoft
exclufively, the traffic of the world.

What

What the Phœnicians were, in early times, relatively to the nations on the Mediterranean coaft; what the Hanfe Towns and the Dutch lately were, relatively to the other European ftates; the commercial towns all over Europe are, at this day, relatively to the reft of the earth. The maritime efforts of the Greeks leffened the importance of Phœnicia. The maritime efforts of the Englifh, and of other powers, have funk the importance of the Dutch commonwealth. The fall of Europe will mark, perhaps, at fome future æra, the enterprize of the fpecies at large; or Europe may only feem to fall, while fhe advances to more abfolute greatnefs, and fuperior opulence, though of lefs relative importance in the political fcale.

But to return to early times: Carthage, a colony planted by the Phœnicians, and inheriting the commercial genius of the parent ftate, flourifhed by the fame arts,

2   and

and grew superior to all nations in naval power. Content with the empire of the sea alone, she might have bid defiance, on that element, to the arms of Rome. But the neglect of her marine, the consequence of a long struggle for dominion on the continent of Europe, rendered her vulnerable on her own coasts. More attentive to the levying of armies, composed chiefly of foreign mercenaries, than to the equipment of fleets, in which alone her genius was peculiarly formed to excel, she allowed a maritime ascendancy to a powerful rival. And, in these circumstances, the jealousy of other states, and intestine divisions, co-operated with the Roman vengeance and ambition in the extinction of the Carthaginian name.

Corinth, situated on an isthmus, in the centre of Greece, and equally connected with the Ægean and Ionian shores, is an example of a city which united with signal advantages

advantages for navigation thofe of inland trade. It derived accordingly, from fo fortunate a coincidence, wealth, fplendor, and magnificence. As a mart of trade, it was no lefs reforted to than Carthage itfelf. They have been called, emphatically, the two eyes of the Mediterranean coaft, and were deftroyed in one year by the Romans. The city of Corinth was reftored by Julius Cæfar; the city of Carthage, by Auguftus. But it was not poffible to reftore, under the Roman yoke, that combination of circumftances which had rendered illuftrious the antient poffeffors of the fame fettlements. Corinth was no longer the capital of a little monarchy, furrounded by free ftates, eminent for arts and fciences. And the new city of Carthage, in the form of a Roman colony, gives us no idea of that city which had been the pride of Africa, and the envy of Rome.

The

The afpiring genius of the Roman people was not formed for commercial arts. During the firft ages of the commonwealth they remained totally unacquainted with maritime affairs. A Carthaginian galley, driven by accident on the coafts of Italy, prefented them with the firft model of a fhip of war. But when naval armaments appeared to be effential to that plan of univerfal dominion after which they afpired, they became intent upon thefe objects, and purfued them with unremitting ardor and aftonifhing fuccefs. The mercantile fpirit and the love of ingenious arts conducted the Phœnicians, the Carthaginians, and the Greeks, to diftinction and eminence as maritime powers. Among thefe nations trade was the principal aim in navigation; war only a collateral object. But this natural order of things was reverfed at Rome. The martial fpirit alone led to the eftablifhment of a marine, which triumphed

over

over the efforts of all the commercial ftates known in the antient world, and rendered the Romans themfelves in fome degree commercial, when no longer a war-like people. It was the fame fpirit which raifed up fuddenly for Mithridates (for he difclaimed all regard to commercial objects, as beneath his dignity) fuch formidable fleets, as infulted the Romans on their own coafts, when, by the annihilation of rival powers, they feemed to be in full poffeffion of maritime empire.

Sometimes local fituation fuggefts correfpondent defigns of great magnitude and importance. Sometimes defigns fuggefted by other confiderations are hence only conducted to a more brilliant or more fuccefsful iffue. In both thefe ways, in the remote ages of antiquity, the Cretans, the Rhodians, and other ftates, availed themfelves of happy fituations in the purfuits of commercial and civil greatnefs.

U ·

But

But local advantages, fluctuating and precarious, often derive their fole account from the temporary condition of the world. It was hence that, long before the fall of Carthage and of Corinth, in confequence of the difcovery of the Indian fea, Alexandria began to flourifh, and became deftined from that difcovery alone, to be the great emporium of trade between the eaft and weft. Its fituation between Tyre and Carthage was convenient for commanding fome fhare of the lucrative trade of which thefe cities had been fo long poffeffed. Tyre was already no more: and Carthage regarded with a jealous eye the erection of a port, which, under the protection of the king of Macedon, might fupplant her in no fmall degree. To produce this effect, as well as to fecure his conqueft of Egypt, feems to have been the view of Alexander in laying the foundations of his new city. But he perceived not then the fource of its importance. It was his expedition into the Indies alone

which

4

which could have opened his eyes on the profpect of its future grandeur. This forms a memorable epoch. The boundaries of commerce being enlarged, and a maritime correfpondence opened between the Indies and the weftern nations, the commodities of the eaft, which had been ufually carried down the Oxus, and along the Cafpian fea, began to be diverted into the channel of Egypt. The Indian trade indeed remained long inconfiderable ; nor did it abandon of a fudden its antient courfe. But in proportion as this change took place under the Ptolemies, and under the Romans, the refort to Alexandria became confpicuous. In one month, fays Jofephus, it fupplied the treafury of Rome with more riches than all the reft of Egypt fupplied in a year. And from the reduction of Egypt into a Roman province by Auguftus, to the conqueft of that country by the Saracens, a period of above feven-hundred years, the port of Alex-

andria

andria was the moſt noted mart in the world. Nor was it leſs renowned as the ſeat of philoſophy and the liberal arts. In the fall of this city we bewail that of learning itſelf, which underwent, upon that ſpot, the moſt fatal cataſtrophes recorded in the annals of time.

Such ſettlements then, as have been mentioned, combined with the peculiar circumſtances of antiquity, had a diſcernible connexion with commercial and civil arts. As commerce therefore, in the ordinary courſe of things, ſeems to make a people flouriſh; a ſettlement conducive to that end is numbered among the cauſes of public proſperity. Yet commerce itſelf, as miniſtering to luxury, was diſcountenanced by the maxims of antient policy; and on the excluſion of it, Rome, and Sparta, and other antient ſtates ſeem to have propoſed to found their greatneſs. This policy, violent indeed and unnatural, ſuited only the genius

genius of martial and heroic times. Yet from hence it appears, that the complexion and temper of an age, by diverſifying national objects, will diverſify proportionably the inherent advantages of any local eſtabliſhment.

The ſpirit of commerce, which actuates modern ages, has opened a new path of ambition. And though there are diſadvantages inſeparable from this ſpirit; though the detail of modern governments affords a leſs ſplendid theme to the hiſtorian than that preſented in the tranſactions of antiquity; yet the civil and moral order of the world is certainly advanced by this great revolution in the views and proceedings of ſtates.

But if the policy of the antients had been more generally directed to commercial objects, yet their maritime operations, we may obſerve, were neceſſarily circumſcribed: and local advantages, once of high eſti-

U 3 mation,

mation, become afterwards comparatively
of fmall importance, and almoft difappear in
an age when the general ufe of the compafs,
and the various improvements in navigation fo far enlarge the fphere of enterprize,
and maintain an intercourfe between regions the moft remote.

In the progrefs of arts, the local advantages of mankind all over the globe feem to
approach nearer to an equality. There
arife more incentives to rouze the induftry
of nations. And a paffage being opened in
every country for the collective treafures of
the earth, general competition and demand
fecure emoluments and rewards to every
people, more accurately proportioned to the
meafure of active exertions, and the wifdom by which they are directed. Riches
or poverty muft no longer be eftimated by
the pofition of a people on the globe. Art,
if I may fay fo, alters the difpenfation of
nature, and maintains a fort of diftributive
justice

juftice in the divifion of opulence among mankind. Such at leaft would be the tendency of things, if all reftrictions on trade were abolifhed by a concert among nations, calculated for the common benefit of all. But mutual jealoufies derange and encumber their mutual efforts. If, in order to keep in view of the coaft, it was often neceffary for antient navigators to prefer the more tedious to the fhorter voyage, a fimilar neceffity is fuperinduced upon the modern, by the abfurdity of commercial regulations. It is the relative profperity of mankind merely which enters into the views of fovereigns. And no regulation, however beneficial to nations, will ever be eftablifhed, by their unanimous confent, if, by any unequal augmentation of opulence or power, it tends to break the rules of proportion, and affects the order in which thefe nations ftand arranged on the general fcale. But if national monopolies, founded on the jealoufy of fovereigns, may

fometimes,

sometimes, as connected with public security, be vindicated on the maxims of sound policy; yet, surely, no such jealousy can reasonably subsist among communities under the same government. On that government at least, in reason and in justice, they have an equal claim. Yet regulations partial and oppressive we have seen in our days, and are too likely to see, dissolved by violence, which ought to have been dissolved in part by the mature wisdom of enlightened councils. Public reformation indeed must be gradual, and such as the times will bear. What is best in theory is not always attainable in practice: and a wise government will proceed, with caution, in authorizing changes, however just, reasonable, and beneficial to the community at large, that are opposed to prejudices grown inveterate by age. Every approach, however, towards an equal legislation, that can be made without disturbing the public tranquillity, obviates the danger of

of rifing difcontents, and tends ultimately
to the harmony and ftability of civil focieties.

But I enter not into thefe complicated
and nice difcuffions. And with regard to
the tendency of national monopolies, and
the genius of exclufive companies, I will
beg leave to refer my readers for the fulleft
information to *an Enquiry into the Nature
and Caufes of the Wealth of Nations :* a
work which will, probably, in future
times, be referred to in political fcience as
the firft juft and fyftematical account, that
has appeared in any language, of the principles of public œconomy, and the phœno-
mena of commercial ftates.

Befides the influence of commerce, there
are other caufes, in the progrefs of general
improvement, by which the importance of
civil fettlements is materially affected.
The

The encreafe of a people in a barren foil led formerly, by a fpecies of neceffity, to plans of migration, of rapine, or of conqueft. And civilized nations in the antient world were able with difficulty to defend their frontiers, when affailed by hungry and defperate barbarians. But when arts and induftry began to be excited in thofe countries, which, for want of tillage and cultivation, had remained defolate and barren, one caufe began to be removed, which difturbed the repofe of nations. Thus the Danes, and other people in the high northern latitudes, fubfifting lefs precarioufly on the fruits of their own induftry, than their forefathers fubfifted by piracy and war, ceafed to prefs with their incumbent weight the neighbouring ftates, and permitted government to advance throughout the reft of Europe. But if rude armies, as hoftile and fierce as ever iffued from the ftorehoufe of nations, were again to appear on the frontiers of any European ftate, the

conteft

conteft would not be dubious; the affail-
ants only would feel the blow. By the
invention of fire-arms, which has changed
by degrees the whole fyftem of war, there
refides a power of refiftance in every flourifhing ftate, to which the moft furious efforts of rude and defperate heroifm were
oppofed in vain. War is now conducted
at an expence which the exertions of induftry can alone fupply; and that fuperiority in arms which once refided with rude
and poor nations, is transferred in modern
ages to the nations advanced in opulence
and credit. Yet the diffufion of knowledge gradually tends to reduce mankind
more nearly to a level in the enterprizes of
peace and war. And that fingular invention, which feemed calculated for the deftruction of mankind, and which actually
enabled a few adventurers from Europe to
annex a hemifphere to its dominion, tends
in the iffue to render battles lefs bloody,

conquefts

conquefts lefs rapid, and governments more fecure than in any former period.

Upon the whole, we obferve local advantages, which fluctuate in every age, and often owe their exiftence and duration to a train of independent events, to be of the leaft relative moment in the moft flourifhing ftage of the arts and fciences. That intercourfe, however, which navigation opens, though abundantly fufficient for the purpofes of mercantile traffic and exchange, can feldom form between diftant nations fo intimate connexions as arife from vicinity of fettlement. Geographical relation therefore will always be, in fome degree, inftrumental in retarding or accelerating, in every country, the progrefs of civil life. Communities, as well as private perfons, are formed by example. And the character of a people muft bear a refemblance in manners, in genius, and in arts,

arts, to that which predominates in the fyftem with which they are more immediately
connected. Civility and rudenefs being
diftributed like light and darknefs in the
natural world, contiguous nations are often
contemporary in their progrefs and decline: and the more enlightened regions,
tho' always fhifting, form at any one time
a complete and undivided whole fituated
around a common centre. But the various
circumftances hitherto under review, ought
to be confidered rather as occafions of profperous or adverfe fortune, than as direct
caufes of human perfection or debafement.
The former ought, by no means, to be confounded with the latter; nor the local circumftances we have mentioned, with that
more myfterious influence which, reaching
the principles of our nature, is fuppofed to
produce original and conftitutional differences in the human fpecies.

ESSAY

E S S A Y IX.

OF THE RELATION OF MAN TO THE SURROUND-
ING ELEMENTS.

LOCAL circumſtances have been
pointed out as of various import;
as diſſuaſives from, or as incentives to action, as occaſions of ſucceſs or diſappoint-
ment to national enterprize, and as more
or leſs auſpicious to the origin and progreſs
of arts and ſciences. But there is, in the
opinion both of the vulgar and the learned, another and more immediate dependence of the ſpecies on external things;
which, preſiding with various effect over
human nature itſelf, antecedently determine its character.

Our

Our external frame, like every fyftem of matter, is fubject to mechanical laws. It is liable accordingly to annoyance from all the elements; and changes introduced into the body cannot, confiftently with the law of their union, be indifferent to the mind. That ftate of the medium, that temperature of heat and cold, thofe productions of foil and fpecies of aliment which correfpond beft with our corporeal fabric, tend to the freer and more vigorous exercife of all the mental powers. Yet natural hiftorians, who defcribe man as an animal merely, allow him in that capacity fome diftin-guifhing prerogatives. While the elements fwarm with life; while earth, fea, and air are peopled with their proper inhabitants; while different tribes have habitations affigned to them in particular corners of the globe, where alone they can find fubfiftence; man erects for himfelf a manfion in every country, fubfifts on a variety of aliment prepared or unprepared by art,

and

and breathes with equal freedom in the frozen or in the burning zone. Races of animals that exifted in paft times feem now to be totally extinct. The largeft and ftrongeft of quadrupeds, according to M. Buffon, has difappeared in the animal world*; nor does he think it impoffible that, confiftently with the order of nature, animals of one common ftock may have been fo diverfified and transformed by the viciffitudes of the globe, as to conftitute diftinct fpecies. The animals of the new and of the old continent may have had one common original; and perhaps of man alone it can be faid in the ftricteft fenfe,

Genus immortale manet ———

The human frame at leaft is more fixed and immutable than any other; and more exempted from that influence which pre-

---

* Hift. Nat. tome xviii. p. 178.

vails

vails through the gradations of animal and vegetable life [A].

There is no one country on the face of the earth which is declared, by general consent, to be the fitteft refidence for man. That influence of the heavens feems to be relatively the beft, which habit has rendered the moft familiar. And to exchange of a fudden one climate for another, is always hazardous for any tribe or people. Yet the pofitive malignancy of no climate of the world can be inferred from the dangers which are fo often confequent on the migrations of mankind. Our phyfical habits are eftablifhed or diffolved by flow degrees; violent tranfitions feem repugnant to nature, and often threaten our conftitution with deftruction. But if it can refift the impetuofity of the fhock, the body accommodates itfelf by degrees to its new condition. Things offenfive become indif-

ferent,

ferent, or even agreeable.; things noxious, innocent, or falutary, and in time perhaps fo effential that no danger were more to be apprehended than a return to antient habits. Emigrants can learn only from experience the peculiarities of other climates ; and, in the courfe of that experience, they ftruggle with a feries of calamity, from which the natives of thofe climates are exempt, and from which the pofterity of thofe emigrants will be exempt in all fucceeding generations. If we may judge then from the firft impreffions on our animal œconomy, the external conftitution of nature in the different climates of the earth tends rather to difcourage than to promote the diftant migrations of mankind. Yet, in another view, it is this diverfity of climate which accounts for the difperfion of nations, and the general revolutions of conqueft. In a flourifhing period indeed of civil and commercial arts, a nation can

hardly

be encumbered with exceffive population. But the more fimple ages are unacquainted with fuch variety of refources. Bold adventure is ever more welcome to barbarians, than the flow proceedings of art; and they even fcorn to accomplifh by induftry what valour alone may effect. In this fpirit was the anfwer of Brennus to the Romans when queftioned, at the fiege of Clufium, concerning his pretenfions on Tufcany*, " That his pretenfions lay in his " fword; and all things belonged to the " brave." He added alfo on more plaufible foundations, after reminding the Romans of fome paffages in their own ftory, that lands which remained neglected, and which the natives were in no condition to cultivate, could not be faid to be exclufively pre-occupied or appropriated by any people. In an exigency then, like that of the Tranfalpine Gauls, it is natural for rude ftates to fend forth colonies to people, or

* Tit. Liv. l. v. c. 36.

armies

armies to fubdue the earth. And the incumbrance from population, which forms
fuch an exigency, will be chiefly felt in the
feverer climates, and in the moſt ungrate-
ful foil. Hence, in later times, the irrup-
tion of the northern barbarians who defo-
lated and fubdued Europe. Their numbers, encreaſing faſter than their induſtry or
the productions of the foil could keep pace
with, created a fpecies of neceffity which,
fuperior to all other confiderations, authorized their firſt movements. And the fortune of the firſt adventurers, by raiſing
expectation, inſtigated others to run a
fimilar career. It deferves however to be
remarked, that the firſt hoſtile incurſions
into a foreign country, have been ufually
made for the fake of plunder merely, without any defign of abandoning antient poffeffions, or of forming new eſtabliſhments.
The firſt inroads of the Barbarians into the
Roman empire were conducted with this

X 3

view

view alone. But the defolation of one territory led to the defolation of another more
remote; till at length a long abfence from
home reconciled thefe foldiers of fortune to
other climes; or the difficulties and dangers of a return, or the temptations of fuperior affluence, retained them in countries
more fertile than their own, better cultivated, and more adorned. No longer content with plunder, they feized upon the
domains of the people fubdued by their
victorious arms; and erected governments
on new foundations, with little regard to
the policy of the vanquifhed. Free in
their own country, they maintained their
freedom in the fettlements they acquired;
armies were transformed into nations; and
feudal fyftems began to arife out of the arrangements of war. The connexions with
the parent ftate were gradually diffolved.
And the pofterity of thofe emigrants, regardlefs of the country of their fore-fa-
thers,

thers, adhered to the governments whofe protection they enjoyed, and to the climates which gave them birth.

Such migrations and eftablifhments refulted from a condition of fociety, to which no European ftate is likely to return for ages. Switzerland perhaps alone is conftituted in fuch circumftances as feem to require a regular difcharge of citizens. Yet, without arts, without manufactures, without money, fhe has eftablifhed a fpecies of commerce peculiar to herfelf, and actually derives from the numbers of her people the means of fubfiftence. She reforts not, like antient ftates, to migrations, to plunder, or to conqueft. While fhe cultivates peace, fhe fubfifts by war; whofe demands fhe fo readily fupplies by hiring out troops indifcriminately to the neighbouring ftates; and this ftrange policy of government is both the caufe and the effect of a flourifhing popula-

X 4

tion.

tion. But if the general circumftances of the modern refembled thofe of the antient world, the Helvetic body, deftitute of fuch refources, could difencumber itfelf by no other expedients than migrations and offenfive war.

Upon the whole then we may obferve, that the changes of fituation on the furface of the globe, fo incident to tribes and nations, far from authorizing any plea of local pre-eminence, ferve only to demonftrate the latitude allowed to the human conftitution in refpect of the variety of climate and of aliment which correfponds fo happily with its texture.

The power of the human body to redrefs itfelf, when annoyed by the elements, is often aftonifhing. Under alterations of the medium more violent, more fudden, more oppofite than climate ever prefents, it maintains an almoft incredible equality in

its

its own temperature. It appears from a feries of late experiments*, conducted by a fociety of gentlemen every way qualified to inform the Public, that, when furrounded with air heated to 244° on the fcale of Fahrenheit, the heat of the animal body deviates but little from its natural ftandard. In the conduct too of thefe curious experiments, as well as in the unfolicited experience of ordinary life, is difplayed the tendency of habit to correct and mitigate the effects of external annoyance.

If it is not then intenfity alone, but rather viciffitude of temperature, which is moft apt to annoy our frame; it would feem even reafonable to infer, that nations commonly reputed the moft fubject to impreffions from the external elements, are in reality the moft exempt from their do-

* See Experiments by Charles Blagden, M. D. F. R. S. inferted in Phil. Tranf. for 1775.

minion;

minion; and that it is not in our variable and inconftant climates, but under a more permanent and equal fky, that we ought to look for the freer and more uninfluenced condition of the fpecies.

On the other hand, it might be contended that viciffitude itfelf, when regular and progreffive, like the return of the feafons, becoming familiar to the body, fhocks or incommodes it in an inferior degree; and that no one ftate of the atmofphere, in our temperate zones, has fuch intenfity and duration as to produce fenfible effects on the human frame.   Without entering at prefent into fo nice a problem, let it be fufficient to obferve, that habit and violent tranfition, exclufively of other influence, account for a number of appearances.   But it is not pretended they account for all; and how nicely foever advantages and difadvantages may be balanced upon the

whole,

whole, there are at leaft fome diftinctions among mankind infallibly regulated
by a local ftandard.

In fome climates of the world, the body
arrives foon at maturity, and haftens to a
diffolution with proportionable celerity.
In other climates a longer period is allowed
both for its progrefs and decline. In the
ages of antiquity the Britons were remarkable for the longeft, the Egyptians for the
leaft extended life; while the ordinary
ftandard in other countries deviated, as was
fuppofed, more or lefs from thefe oppofite
extremes. Confiftently with the fame
order of fecond caufes, modern hiftory in-
forms us of a variety of people among
whom the natural term of life exceeds not,
or even falls below the ftandard of Egypt;
and the Britons yield, perhaps, in longe-
vity to the more northern nations. The
balance of numbers indeed may not be
affected

affected by fuch diftinctions. If climates the moft prolific are alfo the moft deftructive to the human fpecies, the rules of proportion are not broken ; and the encreafe of mankind in one country may be as effectually advanced by the prolongation of life, as in another by a more abundant progeny. But, whether the law of mortality be fo adjufted or not to the law of generation, the ftated period of life is fomewhat variable among nations. And, if the facts were doubtful or equivocal in general hiftory, the influence in this refpect of local fituations, and of air of different temper, might be afcertained from the public regifters of mortality in contiguous fettlements, and under the fame civil œconomy. The air of the Hague is reputed the beft in Holland : the air of Amfterdam the moft malignant : and the duration of life in thofe two places, feems to correfpond with this natural caufe. To correct fuch influences, there is perhaps fome fovereign antidote,

tidote, fome controuling regimen laid up, for future generations, in the ftores of phi-lofophy. But from fact to poffibility there lies no appeal; and in all ages of the world, the term of our exiftence, though depend-ent on a multiplicity of caufes, feems to have had fome reference to climate; and in general to have increafed with the latitude. Strength and vigour of body, till we arrive at the limit of the Polar circle, are found to encreafe in a fimilar progreffion.

Stature and magnitude, on the other hand, are at leaft as confiderable in the warmer as in the colder regions. And the moft diminutive and dwarfifh of the hu-man race are perhaps the natives of the frigid zone.

The Patagonian ftature, after exercifing fo long the curiofity, the fcepticifm, the credulity of the public, is at laft fufficiently

afcertained,

afcertained, and feems not to violate, in any marvellous degree, the ufual defcription of man. But, as a contraft to this, the world has been lately amufed with an account of a nation, in the ifland of Madagafcar, where the ordinary ftature rifes not above three feet and a half. It is not, however, pretended that the Patagonians are eminent for intellectual abilities above other tribes of Barbarians ; and the little people of Madagafcar feem to have nothing dwarfifh in the conftitution of their minds. They are defcribed, by an intelligent writer*, as a warlike people, and a match in genius, in conduct, and in enterprize, for the other natives of the ifland. Yet, without impeaching fo refpectable authority, we may be permitted to obferve, that probably the fame illufion of imagination which magnified the dimenfions of the human figure in

* Eloge de M. Commerfon par M. de la Lande.

Patagonia,

Patagonia, has diminifhed them in Madagafcar. And the only admiffible conclufion is, that in the one country as in the
other, there prevails a remarkable deviation
from the ufual ftandard towards oppofite
extremes.

The exiftence of fuch varieties in the defcription of man is conformable to hiftory,
and to experience, and is in part deducible
from analogy and philofophic theory.
But fuch varieties, though refulting from the
general and regular tenour of mechanical
laws, afford no criterion by which to afcer-
tain the endowments of the underftanding
among tribes or nations. Among the
natives of the fame fpot fimilar diftinctions
abound, exclufive of all apparent connexion
with temper, with genius, or with capacity.
No hiftorian has defcribed that meafure of
animal ftrength, that fymmetry of outward
form, or that natural term of exiftence,
which,

which, in the courfe of human life, is found
moft connected with the largeft endowments
and accomplifhments of the fpecies. In
every age and country thefe combinations
and affemblages are too diffimilar and various to form the bafis of any theory : or
rather, fuch diffimilarity and variety demonftrate the indifference of nature with
regard to fuch co-incidences in the fyftem
of man. Yet the hiftory of human reafon
is liable to be confounded with the hiftory
of mere animal diftinctions ; as if national
genius or capacity could be calculated from
the bills of mortality, from the gradations
of colour in different tribes, or from certain varieties in organical texture which,
being either foreign to the mind, or correfponding equally with all its perfections
and infirmities, touch not the effentials of
human greatnefs.

The Tartars and Chinefe, between whom
there is obferved by travellers, an exact refemblance

femblance in all the lineaments and proportions of the body, difcover little affinity
in the genius or complexion of the mind;
or rather, the refemblance in the one refpect is not more confpicuous than the
contraft in the other. The former people
are defcribed as bold, warlike, independent, lovers of toil, and of a ferocity
approaching to brutality. The latter, as
an indolent and pacific race, prone to fuperftition, and to fervile dependence ; addicted
to compliment, and extravagant in all the
ceremonials of behaviour. Thus the extremes of national character may be combined with exterior appearances nearly
fimilar.

It is alfo worthy of obfervation, that palpable defects in the animal conftitution coincide fo often with the perfection of the
underftanding; and palpable defects in the
intellectual, with the utmoft perfection in

Y   all

all the animal powers. Some illuftrious examples of fuch coincidences occur among the characters of the laft age : an age, perhaps, as fertile of intellectual talents as the world has ever feen. One of thefe is Lord Falkland, whofe difadvantages in perfon are contrafted with excellence of mind by the noble hiftorian who has delivered his name down to pofterity as a model of perfection. Another is Sir Charles Cavendifh, whofe character, as delineated by the fame mafterly hand, conveys a moral leffon to pofterity [B].

The *Graces*, according to the fine allufion of antiquity, are often to be contemplated under the form of the *Satyrs*. Such coincidences, which abound in every country, feem to announce the peculiar character of the human mind, its independence on the laws of mechanifm, and its alliance with a nobler fyftem.

A dif-

A difregard of this high prerogative has contaminated, in fome inftances, the conduct of nations. Hence the policy of Sparta authorifed an inftitution the moft fhocking in the proceedings of mankind; that inftitution of Lycurgus, by which children of a delicate frame were condemned to inftant death, from a fuppofed connexion between intellectual and corporeal infirmity. How different is the wifdom of nature, which ufually renders fuch children the darling objects of parental care!

Had the Spartan rule been adopted in our age, England had not reared up a Lyttelton, nor Europe bred a Voltaire. But, in the eye of reafon and philofophy, this connexion difappears; and a policy fo repugnant to the firft dictates of morality, derives no countenance or apology from the hiftory of individuals or of tribes. If there fubfifts then no infeparable connexion, no

neceffary

neceſſary or eſtabliſhed harmony between the perfections of body and·mind, the·inferences from analogy are deſtitute of ſolid foundation; and the changes introduced into the former by external·impulſe, will imply no correſponding changes in our moral frame.

Soil and climate ſeem to act with a gradation of influence on vegetable, animal, and intellectual nature. There are varieties of configuration, equally commodious for the animal functions; and varieties in our animal powers equally conſiſtent with the exertion of all the nobler faculties. Man, therefore, by his rank in the creation, is more exempted from mechanical dominion than the claſſes below him; and even the beauty of his perſon derives its arbitrary eſtimation from the variety of which the body is ſuſceptible, without detriment to its functions. An exalted mind in a well-organized

organized body, is like a fine picture in a good light. Yet the exterior mechanifm may be regarded, in fome refpects, as the mere drapery of nature, wherein is difplayed all the wantonnefs of art; and which is ufually no more decifive of the abfolute perfections of mankind, than the modes of artificial attire. But the attire of nature, like the fafhions of art, may prove cumberfome and incommodious, not only for animal but for intellectual exertions; and certain confequences will arife from that myfterious union which enters into fo complicated an exiftence, and connects it with the vegetable and with the animal world.

- It deferves alfo to be obferved, that the rank of man, which in fo many refpects renders his conftitution fuperior to dangerous annoyance, renders it in one refpect more vulnerable. An animal feels only what difturbs the animal œconomy. The

fcenery

fcenery of creation it regards with total
indifference ; but that fcenery acts on a human being in a peculiar manner, and without annoying his perfon, affects the fenfibility and delicacy of his moral frame. The organs of found and fight are fufceptible of
impreffions which, exclufive of all arbitrary
affociations or convention, intereft in an
eminent degree the imagination and the
paffions. Hence the elements of natural
language. Hence a moral expreffion in
mufic. Hence certain graces of proportion, figure, motion ; and all the fine connexions which form the foundations of
criticifm in the elegant and polite arts.

The objects with which the fenfes are
converfant, become emblematical to the
imagination, and call forth a train of correfponding emotions, which are never excited in the inferior orders of animal
life.

Some

Some predominant qualities in rude and
favage tribes are to be afcribed, in the opinion of ingenious writers, to the face of
the country they inhabit. The emotions
in the breaft of the favage derive, it feems,
a degree of wildnefs and ferocity from the
chaos which furrounds him ; and a certain adjuftment and embellifhment of the
outward objects is requifite to difpel the
gloom of life, to enliven and exhilarate the
fpirits, to mollify the temper, and to render it humane.

———— The attentive mind,
By this harmonious action on her pow'rs,
Becomes herfelf harmonious.

But this adjuftment is not equally indifpenfable throughout the habitable globe.
For, independently of culture, the fcene
from the hand of nature is more or lefs
magnificent, more or lefs adorned. Here are
immenfe deferts ; there delicious plains.

This

This the region of clouds and storms; that of a more placid and benignant sky. Here predominates the beautiful; there the sublime. The emotions hence generated correspond; and the tone of temper and of manners is, if I may say so, in unison with the natural world. This species of energy, which rises out of external things, exerts itself in its full effect on man alone; and seems to be attended with consequences in rude and savage life, analogous to those which result in the progress of society, from various style and composition in the imitative and designing arts.

Having thus stated the relations of man to the elements around him, which appear to be various and complicated, it will be proper to contemplate his resources, and to mark those distinguishing prerogatives by which he endeavours

vours to maintain or to reſtore his independence, to re-act upon external things,
and to become, in ſome degree, the arbiter of his own happineſs and perfection.

NOTES.

NOTES.

Note [A], p. 306.

THE privileges of man as an animal are incontestible, and wonderfully adapted to his superior rank in the creation. Nous trouverons, says Monf. Buffon with equal truth and elegance, nous trouverons que l'homme est le seul des êtres vivans dont la nature soit assez forte, assez etendue, assez flexible pour pouvoir subsister, se multiplier par-tout, et se preter aux influences de tous les climats de la terre; nous verrons evidemment qu'aucun des animaux n'a obtenu ce grand privilege; que loin de pouvoir se multiplier par-tout, la plupart font bornés et confinés dans des certains climats, et même dans des contrées particuliéres. L'homme est en tout l'ouvrage du ciel; les animaux ne font à beaucoup d'egards que des productions de la terre.

Hist. Nat. Tome xviii. p. 177.

Other distinctions might be mentioned no less conspicuous. Nature has fixed certain seasons

6   at

at which the greater part of the animal kind propagate their feveral fpecies : while a fimilar prerogative is vefted in man at all feafons, and in all climates of the world.

Vide Ariftot. de Hift. Animal. l. v. c. 8.

This diftinction, in the fchool of Socrates, was infifted on as an argument for a fuperintending providence. To δε, faid that mafter of wifdom, και τας των αφροδισιων ηδονας τοις μεν αλλοις ζωοις δαναι, περιγραψαντας τ8 ετ8ς χρονον, ημιν δε συνεχως μεχρι γηρως ταυτας παρεχειν. Xenoph. Mem. l. i. c. 4. " Is it not well ordered, " that, while the courtfhips of the grove are " confined to one period of the year, the period " of our loves is not thus interrupted, and is " prolonged to declining age ?"

Note [B], p. 322.

I WILL beg leave to lay before the reader the eminent and worthy character mentioned in the text, as it is drawn by the moft inftructive, and perhaps the moft faithful hiftorian of the laft age. " The converfation, " fays Clarendon, fpeaking of himfelf, the Chan-" cellor took moft delight in, was that of Sir " Charles

" Charles Cavendish, brother to the Marquis,
" who was one of the most extraordinary per-
" fons of that age, in all the noble endowments
" of the mind. He had all the disadvantages
" imaginable in his person, which was not only
" of so small a size, that it drew the eyes of
" men upon him; but with such deformity in
" his little person, and an aspect in his counte-
" nance, that was apter to raise contempt than
" application: but in this unhandsome or
" homely habitation, there was a mind and a
" soul lodged that was very lovely and beauti-
" ful; cultivated and polished by all the know-
" ledge and wisdom that arts and sciences could
" supply it with. He was a great philosopher
" in the extent of it, and an excellent mathe-
" matician, whose correspondence was very
" dear to Gassendus and Descartes, the last of
" whom dedicated some of his works to him.
" He had very notable courage, and the vigour
" of his mind so adorned his body, that being
" with his brother the Marquis in all the war,
" he usually went out in all parties, and was
" present, and charged the enemy in all battles
" with as keen a courage as could dwell in the
" heart of man. But then the goodness of his
" disposition, the humility and meekness of his
                                        " nature,

" nature, and the vivacity of his wit was admi-
" rable. He was fo modeft, that he could
" hardly be prevailed with to enlarge himfelf on
" fubjects he underftood better than other
" men, except he were preffed by his very fa-
" miliar friends, as if he thought it prefump-
" tion to know more than handfomer men
" ufe to do. Above all, his virtue and piety
" was fuch, that no temptation could work
" upon him to confent to any thing that fwerved
" in the leaft degree from the precife rules of
" honour, or the moft fevere rules of confci-
" ence." Life of Clarendon, Vol. III.

Thus far the noble hiftorian, who in the laft
feature of the character feems to have drawn,
by anticipation, the Cavendifhes of our days;
whofe inflexible integrity and patriotifm appear in the Britifh fenate; and whofe hereditary
virtues are worthy of the houfe of Cavendifh,
and of the former age.

ESSAY

" nature, and the severity of his wit we admire
" able. The spirit of ... man ... and
" hardly be provoked ... to render himself un-
" agreeable to persons of a better ... than other
" ... were; he hare excelled by his very be-
" nefiter towards ... of his friends. If you long
" ... do I know ... more humiliation that
" there are. Alas ... the virtues and glory
" of ... think, that no temp ... considerab ...
" upon life to content to my thing that I loved
" with the least desire from the people rules of
" ... it, or ... mode ... the ... life of our ...
" ... *Life of Cicero*, Vol. III.

That ... this ... situation, at the height of
Balzac of the ministers seem to have been a
... ... the ... the duvresses of Cicero ...
... ... that in one opinion ... er ... ...
... ... little ... ... which in a ther ...
... ... Caesar.

ESSAY

OF MAN, AS THE ARBITER OF HIS OWN FORTUNE.

NATURAL and moral ills are effential to our fyftem. It is in vain to
enquire into their origin. An exemption
from the former would imply phyfical independence; an exemption from the latter,
all moral perfection. Such attributes are
divine. Yet man is neither chained down
by neceffity, nor impelled by fate. And
refignation to the unalterable order of
things, a fentiment fo becoming his
condition, ought not to arreft the hand
of induftry, or to contract the fphere
of active enterprize. After all the efforts he can boaft, after exhaufting

the

the accumulated exertions of ages, there remains, and will remain, abundant fcope for all the paffive virtues in the life of man. Let him then fuftain with dignity the weight of his condition; yet not meanly acquiefce in grievances within his province to redrefs.

The action of the elements on his frame is not more confpicuous, than his reciprocal action on thofe very elements which are permitted to annoy his being. He has a range allowed him in the creation peculiar to himfelf alone; and he feems to have had delegated to him a certain portion of the government of the natural world. Revolutions, indeed, are brought about in various regions by the univerfal laws of motion, uncontrouled, and uncontroulable by any human power. But, under certain limitations, foil and climate are fubject to his dominion; and the natural hiftory of the terraqueous

terraqueous globe varies with the civil hiftory of nations.

´ In the defcriptions of antient and modern Europe, the fame countries appear to be ef-fentially different. The climates beyond the Atlantic are altered fince the days of Co-lumbus. But fuch differences and altera-tions are more rightly imputed to the con-duct and operations of men, than to any mutability in the courfe of nature. Nor are fuch alterations confined to thofe fettle-ments on which the additional culture has been beftowed. The arts of tillage and agriculture have a more diffufive and ge-neral effect. The country of Italy, though not better cultivated than in the days of the Romans, has undergone fince thofe days a viciffitude of temperature, which has arifen, in all probability, from the more improved flate of Germany and France.

Z   The

The temperature of climates throughout America, so different from that which predominates under the same parallels of latitude in the antient world, is not entirely to be ascribed to fixed and permanent causes, but rather to the more recent existence of nations in the new hemisphere, and the inferior cultivation it has consequently received from the hand of man. Thus much is certain: by opening the soil, by clearing the forests, by cutting out passages for the stagnant waters, the new hemisphere becomes auspicious, like the old, for the growth and population of mankind.

Let us learn then to wage war with the elements, not with our own kind; to recover, if one may say so, our patrimony from Chaos, and not to add to his empire.

The history of the colonies, and commercial establishments of the European nations,

tions, teſtifies that, in almoſt every corner, a healthful and ſalubrious climate is the ſure effect of perſevering and well-conducted labour. Nor is the oppoſite effect chargeable merely on the neglect of culture, and the atmoſphere that overhangs the deſert alone malignant. The malignancy is often directly chargeable on manners, on police, and on civil eſtabliſhments. In ſome of the moſt malignant climates on the Guinea coaſt, the impure habits of the natives have been aſſigned as the efficient cauſe. The exhalations of a negro village, negroes only can endure.

" The plague, ſays Dr. Chandler in his
" Travels into the Eaſt, might be wholly
" averted from theſe countries, or at leaſt
" prevented from ſpreading, if lazarettos
" were erected, and ſalutary regulations
" enforced, as in ſome cities of Europe.
" Smyrna would be affected as little per-

" haps

" haps as Marfeilles, if the police were as
" well modelled. But this is the wifdom
" of a fenfible and enlightened people."

A fpecies of neceffity, however, in fome
countries conducts mankind to certain deco-
rums in life and manners, which wait, in
other countries, the ages of tafte and refinement. The Dutch certainly are not the moft
polite among the European nations ; yet the
nature of their civil fettlement, as if anticipating the dictates of refinement, introduced
among them from the beginning, a degree
of order in their police, and of cleanlinefs in
their houfehold œconomy, not furpaffed, perhaps unequalled, by any other people. On
a principle of health, an attention to cleanlinefs is more or lefs incumbent on all communities. It prefents an emblem of inward
purity, and is dignified, perhaps not impro-
perly, in fome fyftems of ethics, with the
appellation of a moral virtue. But with
all

all imaginable precaution on this fcore, the confluence of numbers in a crowded fcene is generally productive of difeafe. Hence peftilential diftempers are fo often bred in the camp, and ufually march in the train of war. And hence the eftablifhment of great cities, under the beft regulated police, can be demonftrated, from the bills of mortality, to be deftructive in a high degree of population and public health*. But all thefe examples relate to artificial, not to natural climate; and there feems to be little ground, in the hiftory of the terraqueous globe, to affociate with any fixed and immutable conftitution of the atmofphere, the happinefs or perfections of the human fpecies [A]. Yet local prejudices every where abound : the moft accomplifhed citizens in nations and ages the moft accomplifhed, have not been exempted from their fway.

* See Dr. Price's Obfervations on Reverfionary Payments.

Z 3

Plato

Plato returned thanks to the immortal Gods that he was an Athenian, not a Theban born; that he breathed on the southern, not on the northern side of the Asopus. But if Athens was eminent for refinement, there were other causes than the climate. And, if the Bœotians were dull to a proverb, it was a temporary calamity, and Pindar, and Pelopidas, and Epaminondas shall vindicate the soil. Thus much we may with certainty affirm, that soil and climate, if not altogether foreign to the mind, are, like the mind, susceptible of improvement, and variable, in a high degree, with the progress of civil arts. Settlements abandoned by one colony, have been re-peopled with success by another. Projects thought desperate in days of ignorance, have been resumed and conducted to a prosperous issue in more enlightened times. Individuals have often failed in their attempts, for want of public encouragement.

Public

4

Public enterprizes have failed for want of concurrence among nations. Eftablifh then concert and union among mankind; all regions become habitable, and the elements almoft ceafe to rebel.

Nor is this command over the elements the only effect of progreffive induftry and labour. The changes introduced into clothing, fubfiftence, modes of life, prefent confiderations of equal moment. In confequence of thefe changes, our animal fituation is as fluctuating as our moral; and the fame people, in the ages of rudenefs and civility, will retain fewer marks of refemblance in their organical ftructure, than will be found among the moft diftant nations when contemplated in correfponding points of their progrefs. A people emerged above the wilder ftates, who fubfift by the culture of the foil, not by its fpontaneous provifion; who farther fuperadd the

ufe

use of foreign commodities to the domestic articles of confumption, have undergone tranfitions, gradual perhaps and infenfible, but which have affected their whole animal œconomy. Thus the commercial arts, by concentring in one corner of the world the divided treafures of the earth, confound the primeval diftribution and arrangement of things, and diverfify in the fame climate the condition of tribes and nations. There feems to be a certain regimen of life fuited to the local circumftances of mankind, which is fuggefted to them at firft by inftinct, or is the flow refult of experience. A different regimen, recommended in a fimilar manner, is beft adapted to their circumftances in another region; and fudden or injudicious alterations in the modes of life are among the fatal confequences that attend the commerce of nations. The transference too of epidemical diftemper from region to region is another confequence

quence of that commerce no lefs deftructive. Diftempers, local in their origin,
being thus diffufed over the globe, become,
when tranfplanted, more formidable than in
their native feats. The plague, fo defolating
when it invades Europe, commits not
equal havoc in the eaft. The malady, im-
ported by Columbus, was lefs virulent in
the American climates. On the other
hand, the fmall-pox, introduced into thofe
climates by the Europeans, threatened the
depopulation of the new hemifphere.

Time, however, which corrects the effects
of migrations, feems alfo to correct the vi-
rulence of tranfplanted diftemper. Either
the human conftitution oppofes it with new
vigour, or the art of medicine combats it
with more fuccefs ; or the poifon, by being
long blended with the furrounding elements, ceafes to be fo deftructive. It may
alfo be obferved, that fome diforders leave

impreffions

impreffions in the conftitution which prevent
in future the poffibility of fimilar annoyance.
Hence the expediency of inoculation, a
practice firft introduced into Europe from
the eaft, which folicits difeafe through a
fafer channel, as a prefervative againft its
eventual attack in all the circumftances of
its natural malignity. But to return from
this digreffion, let us furvey the farther
tendency of the commercial arts.

The natural productions of one corner
fupply the demands of luxury in another,
and the moft diftant tribes may approxi-
mate each other in their animal temperament by mutual traffic. Even the natives
of the moft penurious foil may exchange
the rude fimplicity of their anceftors for the
extravagance of the moft pampered nations.
As national affluence, however, is not diftributed equally among the feveral members
of the community (for under an equal divifion

vifion of property no government can long
fubfift) we often obferve at once, in the
diftinction of ranks, fuch effects of various
temperament as arife in fucceffion to the
public from the general viciffitudes of fociety. Penury and wealth, fimplicity and
prodigality, indolence and toil, create conftitutional diftinctions among the different
orders of citizens. For the impreffion of
the commercial arts is often confpicuous in
the upper departments of life, before it
reaches thofe of inferior condition; but
the circle gradually widens. The exclufive
poffeffion of opulence cannot be long maintained; and the fluctuation, fo natural to
commercial ftates, muft diffeminate the effects over the public at large.

In the laft period of the Roman government, the different provinces of the empire
became contaminated with the luxury of
the eaft, whofe influence on the bodily
temperament

temperament may have contributed, along with moral and political diſtemper, to the ſucceſs of the northern armies.

—————————Sævior armis
Luxuria incubuit, victumque ulciſcitur orbem.

But theſe ſymptoms of decay, which ſpread at laſt over the provinces, and tainted the maſs of the people, had originated among the nobles, and in the ſeat of government. It was the legions, not the ſenate, the pro-vincials, not the Romans, who acted, during ſeveral generations, as the maſters of mankind. Aurelian, and Probus, and Dioclefian, the reſtorers of the Roman world, were not of Roman blood. And Rome, more debauch-ed than the diſtant provinces, had ſeen ſome of them, ages before her fall, erected into diſtinct and independent ſtates, no longer acknowledging her ſovereign authority, or the laws of the empire.

Such

Such confequences, however, imply no imputation on the arts of civil life. The food, the raiment, the occupations of the polifhed citizen may be as innocent as thofe of the favage. The latter is even guilty of exceffes which difappear in the age of refinement. The immoderate ufe of intoxicating liquors is generally moft predominant in the ruder forms of fociety. It is relinquifhed in the progrefs of refinement, and feems to be fcarce compatible with the elegant luxuries of a highly cultivated people.

A propenfity indeed to vicious excefs may be accidentally combined in the fame character with a high relifh for the luxuries of life. But the paffions themfelves are totally diftinct. A pronenefs to luxury, with an averfion to all riot or excefs, is no uncommon character; and a pronenefs to excefs, with an averfion to luxury, though

more

more rare, is by no means without example.

A ſtriking example occurs in the character
of the famous Iriſh rebel, who, in the reign
of Elizabeth, aſſumed the rank and appellation of King of Ulſter. "He was a man,
"ſays the hiſtorian, equally noted for his
"pride, his violence, his debaucheries, and
"his hatred of the Engliſh nation. He is
"ſaid to have put ſome of his followers to
"death, becauſe they endeavoured to in-
"troduce the uſe of bread after the Engliſh
"faſhion. Though ſo violent an enemy
"to luxury, he was extremely addicted to
"riot, and was accuſtomed, after his in-
"temperance had thrown him into a fever,
"to plunge his body into mire, that he
"might allay the flame which he had
"raiſed by former exceſſes *.

* Hiſtory of England, vol. v. p. 399.

Luxury,

Luxury, according to its species and direction, may be pronounced to be either salutary or destructive. By its connexion with industry and active exertion, it is productive of the noblest effects. It is the parent of ingenious arts, and conducts a people to honour and distinction. Yet objects which are not only innocent, but beneficial in the pursuit, may prove dangerous in the possession; and the acquisitions of national virtue may become the occasion of its fall. Habits there surely are, incident to different periods of society, which tend to enervate the body, and to vitiate the blood. The mechanical springs of life rest not on the energy of one cause, but on the combination of many, possessing often opposite and qualifying powers. It were improper therefore to expatiate on the intensity of one principle, without attending to others which serve to heighten or to mitigate its force. One writer magnifies the power of climate; another,

another, the effects of aliment; a third, the
efficacy of labour or reft, and the peculiar
influence of certain modes of life. But
thefe circumftances are relative to each
other, and it is the refult of the combination with which we are alone concerned.
It was well anfwered by the Spartan to the
King of Syracufe, who found fault with the
coarfenefs of the Spartan fare, " In order,
" fays he, to make thefe victuals relifh, it
" is neceffary to bathe in the Eurotas."

By the progrefs of agriculture and rural
œconomy in our climates, that mode of
fubfiftence has become the mofteafy, which
was formerly the moft difficult. And it
were well perhaps for mankind, in moft
countries of Europe at this day, if the great
and opulent exchanged with thofe of inferior condition many of the daily articles of
confumption. Vegetable aliment feems to be
better adapted to the more indolent clafs of
citizens.

citizens. The labouring part of fociety require a larger proportion of animal food. But it is often difficult for the meaner fort to procure for themfelves fuitable fubfiftence, and more difficult for their fuperiors to abftain from improper gratifications.

If I were not Alexander, faid the Prince of Macedon, I would chufe to be Diogenes. Yet the generality of people would rather imitate the conduct of Ariftippus, who, for the pageantry of a court, and the pleafures of a luxurious table, could forego independence, and defcend from the dignity of philofophy to the adulation of Kings [B]. The conduct however of mankind, in uncorrupted times, was more conformable to nature; and their reafon taught them to form fuch habits and combinations as were moft congruous with their external condition. Different fyftems of policy grow out of thefe combinations; and ufages and

A a   laws

laws relative to climate make a capital figure in antient legiflation. Even fuper-ftition, on fome occafions, has proved a guardian of public manners, and a ufeful auxiliary to legiflative power. Abftinence from the flefh of animals, abftinence from wine, frequent purifications, and other external obfervances among the Indians, the Perfians, the Arabians, how abfurd fo-ever if transferred to other countries, form-ed on the occafions, and in the countries where they were inftituted, important branches of political œconomy. The Egyptians prefcribed by law a regimen for their Kings. In fome inftances, cer-tain rules of proportion were eftablifhed; and fuitable to the different claffes of citizens, there was a fpecial allotment of aliment prefcribed by the religion of Brama. The Chriftian difpenfation alone, divine in its origin, and defigned to be univerfal, de-fcends not to local inftitutions; but, leav-ing the details of policy to the rulers of

3   nations,

nations, inculcates only thofe pure and effential doctrines which are adapted to all
climates and governments. Yet the *Vedam*,
the *Shafter*, the *Koran*, and other antient
codes, which afford, in one view, fo ftriking examples of credulity and fanaticifm,
may be regarded, in another, as monuments of human fagacity. Happy had it
been for the world, if the founders of religion and government had feparated, in fuch
cafes, the pure gold from the drofs, and
connived only at illufions connected with
public felicity. It were often happy for
rude tribes, if they were taught a local fuperftition, how abfurd foever in its details,
that tended to preferve the fimplicity of
their morals, and debarred them in many
inftances from adopting foreign cuftoms
and manners. How fortunate would it
have been for the Indian tribes, throughout the continent of North America, if
they had been debarred by the folemn fanc-

tions

tions of a religion, as abſurd as that of Mahomet, from the uſe of intoxicating liquors! a practice derived to them from European commerce, and which contributes,
in the new hemiſphere, more, perhaps, than
any other cauſe, to the deſtruction, and what
is worſe, to the debaſement of the ſpecies.

Our voyages of diſcovery, which in ſome
reſpects are ſo honourable, and calculated
for noble ends, have never yet been happy
for any of the tribes of mankind viſited by
us. The vices of Europe have already contaminated the Otaheitean blood. Whether
the Engliſh or French navigators have
been the firſt authors of the dreadful calamity which now afflicts that race, it is of
little importance to decide. While ſo odious a charge is retorted on each other
by thoſe nations, the natives of the
happy iſland, ſo cruelly abuſed, will have
cauſe

caufe to lament for ages, that any European veffel ever touched their fhores.

Felix, heu nimium felix! fi littora tantum ————

Moral depravity is a fertile fource of phyfical ills to individuals, to families, and to nations. Nor are the ills inherent only in the race which bred the diforder. They fpread from race to race, and are often entailed, in all their malignity, on pofterity. Thus hereditary diftemper has a foundation in the natural, as in the moral world. Nor does this reflect upon eternal juftice, or breed confufion in the univerfe, or derogate from the fum of its perfections. If we are punifhed for the vices, we are rewarded too for the virtues of our fathers. Thefe oppofite principles of exaltation and debafement tend to the equilibrium of the fyftem. They ferve alfo to a farther end; they ferve to draw clofer the ties

A a 3   of

of humanity, to remind us of our duty, by reminding us of the relations of our being; and of thofe indiffoluble connexions and dependencies which unite us with the paft, and will unite us with all fucceeding ages.

N O T E S.

N O T E S.

Note [*A*], p. 341.

OF the efficacy of found regimen in preferving health, under all the variety of
climate to which mankind are apt to be expofed,
there occcurs a memorable example in the late
voyage round the world by Capt. Cook, fo juftly
reprefented to the Royal Society, by his elegant
and learned encomiaft. That navigator, whofe
melancholy fate is, at the moment I am writing,
lamented by all Europe, " with a company of
" 118 men, performed a voyage of three years
" and eighteen days, throughout all the climates
" from 52° north to 71° fouth latitude, with
" the lofs of a fingle man only by difeafe :" a
proportion fo moderate, that the bills of mortality, in no climate or condition of fociety, can
furnifh fuch another example.

Note [*B*], p. 353.

HORACE, indeed, in the fpirit of the
courtier, the poet, and the man of pleafure, approves the temporizing fyftem of Arif-

tippus,

tippus, rather than the auſtere rigour of Diogenes. The pedantry of the latter was ſurely exceſſive. But it was the exceſs of that free,
manly, and independent ſpirit, which is allied to
true glory, and formed the heroiſm of antiquity.

Si prænderet olus patienter, regibus uti
Nollet Ariſtippus;

was the judgment of the cynic; and the re-
ply of Ariſtippus is rather ſmart than ſolid;

———— Si ſcirét regibus uti,
Faſtidiret olus, qui me notat. ————

Hor. l. i. ep. 17.

ESSAY XI.

THE magnitude of external annoyance being variable with the maxims of political œconomy, and the rules of civil life, it is the prerogative of every people to hold the balance of good and evil, and to raife or to deprefs the fcale of their own felicity. To the abufe of this prerogative, not to any unalterable conftitution of things, may be afcribed whatever is moft wretched or humiliating in the condition of human fociety. Abfurdities of various defcription in artificial manners, are often deftructive of health and vigour, and even tend to diveft the

natural

natural form of its fymmetry and perfection.

The cuftom of painting the body with
fuch rude materials as the favage life affords, is a practice which, in the infancy
of fociety, appears to have been almoft
univerfal. It is reforted to at firft as an obvious prefervative againft the inclemency
of the feafons, the impreffions of the fun,
moleftation from infects, or other external
annoyance. But this invention, like every
other, was fufceptible of refinement. No
longer adjufted to the ftandard of conve-
niency alone, it became fubject to the caprice and viciffitude of fafhion; and the
embellifhment of the outward perfon,
which was at firft little attended to, or regarded as a collateral confideration, came
in time to be the principal object. Such
fantaftical decorations are worn as enfigns
of dignity, and ferve as fo many badges of
diftinc-

diftinction among favage tribes. This invention may be traced up to remote antiquity in the cuftoms of the European nations. It was reduced to an art among
the antient Britons; and the Caledonians,
the moft antient inhabitants of the Northern
parts of the ifland, were, from their being
peculiarly addicted to this art, denominated
Picts by the Romans. Not content with
fuch reprefentations as were practicable by
the colouring of paint alone, without detriment to the perfon, thofe rude nations
often infcribed their defigns with a weightier
hand, and by actual incifions into the body
rendered the impreffions indelible. Thus
a practice, at firft innocent, or falutary,
became, by degrees, pernicious; and while
it aimed at farther decoration, or at emblematical expreffion, tended in reality to deform the fpecies.

By the progrefs of fociety, fuch fafhions
have long fince difappeared in Europe.
But,

But, if we survey the condition of rude
nations in various corners of the world, we
find the human frame degraded by customs
still more violent and unnatural.   Nor is it
in the option of individuals to embrace, or
to resist such customs. . The violence is frequently, by the imposition of parents, rendered almost coeval with existence.   The
body, in its infant state, more pliant and
ductile, is more easily divested of its just
proportions, and the limbs and members
are then capable of being moulded into
a variety of unnatural and artificial forms,
impracticable in maturer years. If dis-
tortions, then, of feature and person,
are thus early introduced, more serious and
extensive consequences may possibly arise
from the same source,

When the violence is directed, as among
the Chinese and some other nations, to the
extremities of the body, situated at a dis-
tance from the principal organ of sensation,
the

the effect on the animal œconomy is more
fupportable, and the vitals of the conftitution probably elude the injury; but, unfortunately, the impreffion is often made
where the conftitution is moft vulnerable,
and the more fenfible parts fuftain a fhock
annoying to the whole nervous fyftem.
Among one people, to flatten the dimenfions of the head ; among another, to render it more convex, parents have recourfe
to the moft fhocking expedients of art, and
the natural guardians of infancy become
its chief tormentors. The names by which
certain Indian tribes in North America have
been diftinguifhed, are expreffive of fuch
unnatural characteriftics. The Caraibbes
of the Weft Indies, by contrivances and
applications of art nearly fimilar, have
acquired a caft of phyfiognomy altogether
peculiar. The Indians of Afia are not entirely exempted from the fame odious
abufes ; but the principal feat of the enor-

mity

mity is certain regions of Africa, where the art of disfiguring the human person is, if I may say so, almost the only art which has made such progress among the rude inhabit-ants, as to mark their departure from a state of nature.

In such deplorable fashions, which stifle the voice of nature, the sufferers, and the authors of the sufferings, almost equally claim commiseration. But, to distort the natural form with an avowed purpose of deranging the intellectuals of man, is a conduct so flagitious and enormous as has never stained the manners of savage and untutored tribes; yet, not many ages ago, even this enormity existed in the manners of Europe, where, in various instances, the forming fools for the entertainment of the great, was the ultimate end proposed in mutilating the human figure.

The

The recital of fuch examples fills humanity with horror ; and the poffibility of their exiftence would hardly be admitted in a cultivated period, did not hiftory eftablifh the facts upon inconteftible authority, and number them among the corruptions which are found in fo many focieties of men, to degrade the dignity of our fpecies.

There is a variety of other cuftoms among rude tribes, which take their rife from the illufions of imagination. In obferving the gradations of colour among the races of mankind, our ideas of beauty are often entirely governed, or greatly influenced, by a regard to the moft general form of nature we are accuftomed to contemplate. Among a nation of Blacks, the White; among a nation of Whites, the Black was never the approved complexion. The Hottentots, an ambiguous race, equally allied to either extreme, are at pains to deepen the

fhade

shade of black, as if to maintain a conformity with the prevailing complexion of Africa. On the other hand, the Moors of Barbary, the counterpart of the Hottentots in the northern hemisphere, who possess, like them, the medium of complexion, discover little predilection for either extreme, which is owing probably to an almost equal correspondence with African and European nations. Upon the same principle, the copper colour of the Americans is regarded among them as a criterion of beauty; and it seems to be the object of art, by painting the face with vermilion, to maintain, in all its perfection, the predominant complexion of the Indian race. Even the universal principles of taste, when not duly regulated, may lead to egregious abuse. Unequal degrees of beauty, of elegance, and of strength, enter into the various contexture of the human body; and all attempts are vain to superinduce by vio-

lence

5

lence or art, that perfection which is denied
by nature. Conftitutional blemiſhes or
defects may be heightened by too eager a
defire to aboliſh them; and by the violent
fubſtitution of other proportions and lineaments than are confiſtent with the primeval
configuration of the parts, though more conformable, perhaps, to fome ideal ſtandard
of perfection. But fome of the more flagrant examples of violence done the perſon,
to be met with in the cuſtoms of rude tribes,
are neither authoriſed nor fuggeſted by
any perception of beauty. They are defigned, in reality, to create oppoſite emotions, and are dictated by the ferocity of
warlike people on purpoſe to confound
their enemies by appearances ſcarcely human. The gentler ſex, whoſe conſtant aim
is to improve the beauty of the outward
form, and who fubdue mankind only by
their charms, even in the African climates,
never deviate fo far from nature. In the

B b   iſland

island of Biffao, near to the river Gambia,
the matrons are dreffed in decent attire;
and the perfons of the young, though
without all fort of apparel, are not unadorned. The degrees of embellifhment
indicate rank and condition; and the eldeft
daughter of the reigning monarch is diftinguifhed from the other ladies of the court by
elegance of painting, and the richnefs of
her bracelets. But all the happier refinements of fancy are difregarded in the apparatus of war.

The Giagas, thofe bloody cannibals of
Africa, who are regardlefs of natural as of
moral beauty, affume the moft infernal afpect to render themfelves more formidable
to other tribes. The fame principle authorifes the abufe of perfon among various Indian tribes in North America; and authorifed it, according to the Roman Hiftorian*,

* Tacit. de Mor. Germ.

among

among a tribe of the antient Germans. But an afpect fo tremendous to a foreign enemy, may become venerable among people of the fame tribe. The dignity of the expreffion is more confidered than the deformity of the picture. The beautiful is abforbed in the fublime ; and the fpectacle, how odious foever in itfelf, is endured as defcriptive of the degrees of heroifm and martial valour; virtues chiefly refpected in a rude age.

Religious fanaticifm, it may alfo be obferved, is frequently another fource of the moft wretched debafement. Penances, mortifications, Monkifh feverities, and a number of flagrant obfervances, in the ritual of fuperftition, that annoy our frame, have, to the difgrace of the world, been deemed meritorious in the fight of Heaven ; as if one fpecies of guilt could be expiated by another ; or, as if to deform

and

and abuſe our nature, could ever be acceptable to the author of all beauty and excellence.

But it is not neceſſary to carry our reſearches anxiouſly into the principles which have concurred to the introduction and eſtabliſhment of ſo many abſurd cuſtoms among mankind. It is ſufficient to obſerve, that the cuſtoms themſelves, from what fountain ſoever they flow, are often attended with conſequences no leſs deſtructive than odious. Thus what ariſes from human folly may become undiſtinguiſhable from the original workmanſhip; or rather, certain diſtinctions, at firſt adventitious, may become the characteriſtics of a tribe, and even be in part tranſmiſſible and hereditary to future generations. The cuſtoms indeed under review belong chiefly to an unpoliſhed ſtate of ſociety; but they are often ſucceeded by others of a tendency

                                    ſomewhat

somewhat similar. The swathing of in-
fants, the confinement of dress, and other
absurd practices in our œconomy, unprecedented among barbarians, might be mentioned as counterparts of the same violence
among polished nations. In general, perhaps, the hardy discipline of early times is
more auspicious to health, vigour, and sym-
metry of form, than the more refined culture and softer habits of a luxurious age.
But without running the parallel of public
manners in different periods of civil progrefs, it may be affirmed, that some of the
groffer and more heinous abuses we have
here remarked, are irrecoverably destructive of the human figure, and perhaps re-
motely touch the springs of our intellectual
frame. There being then such a variety
of effects, immediately of physical production, which can be traced up to a moral
original; it is proper to distinguish and separate that order of second causes which is

regulated

regulated by the resolutions and conduct of men, from the independent and immutable influence of external things.

But moral sentiment, exclusive of its breaking forth into action, by its silent and internal movements in the human breast, affects, in no small degree, the beauty, health, and perfection of our organized system; and this connection of things, though more rarely the object of attention, ought not to be overlooked in explaining the diversity of appearances in the various tribes of mankind.

E S S A Y XII.

OF THE TENDENCY OF MORAL CHARACTER TO DIVERSIFY THE HUMAN FORM.

THE mind itſelf is often the original ſeat of diſorder which is transferred to the animal ſyſtem. In the hiſtory of individuals, it is obvious to obſerve, that a diſtempered imagination, and irregular paſſions, frequently prey upon the body, waſte its vigour, and even haſten its diſſolution. Judging then from analogy, it ſeems not unreaſonable to expect, that the paſſions, to which ſociety is occaſionally obnoxious, may be productive of ſimilar effects upon the multitude, appear in exterior ſymptoms, impair the

ſoundneſs

foundnefs of public health, and enervate the principle of animal life. What form of society is moft open to this annoyance, is a problem which, perhaps, the hiftory of the fpecies is not able to refolve. But, in general, it may be pronounced of human life, that the vindictive, the envious, and unfocial paffions are hoftile to the poffeffor, while all the oppofite emotions diffufe a kindlier influence over our animal frame. " How miferable are the damned! faid Saint " Catherine of Genoa; they are no longer " capable of love." So clofe is the focial union, that if the fierceft tyrant that ever exifted in human form was doomed to be himfelf the executioner of his bloody edicts, the victims of his tyranny would become the inftruments of his punifhment, and the torture inflicted would be more than he could endure. The little tyrant of Greece, whom the Hecuba of Euripides chafed from the public theatre, all bathed in tears, retained, in

in defiance of himfelf, the fenfibility of nature. And if the heart is thus liable to be
fubdued by fiction, how fhould it fuftain,
in fimilar circumftances, the actual pre-
fence of woe? To be callous to fuch impreffions, is to be more or lefs than man;
and, even where virtue is extinct, our organized fyftem is liable to be affected by
· this powerful fympathy of minds.

Varieties of national character we obferve
imprinted on the phyfiognomy of nations.
The feveral qualities of levity or vanity,
dignity or pride, pufillanimity, fortitude,
dulnefs, vivacity, ferocity, meeknefs, and a
thoufand nicer gradations of moral character, rife up in the vifage, and mark the
exterior of man. Individuals, it is allowed,
are often found devoid of the characteriftics
that predominate in the family, in the
tribe, or in the nation to which they belong, while they retain, neverthelefs, all
the

the ufual marks of thofe characteriftics.
Hence, phyfiognomy is a delufive art; men
are belied by appearances, till at laft the
genuine expreffion of the individual is in-
terpreted, and declares the fallacy of more
equivocal and general figns. Thefe general figns, the accumulated effect, perhaps, of prevailing habit for generations,
may become congenial to a race; and,
being wrought into the organization, cannot be effaced at once by the abfence of
the caufes which contributed to their formation. To correct, and to eftablifh mental habit, is the prerogative of a moral
agent; but the lineaments and proportions
of the body are not variable with the gradations of intellectual improvement; and
hence the mind is fo often at variance with
the forms which the countenance affumes,
in confequence of its primæval caft. When
the moft exalted genius of antiquity, by
the exertion of this prerogative, had re-
formed

formed and ennobled all the features of his character, a phyfiognomift, by the rules of art, judged of him from his conftitutional propenfities. Some latitude, however, is allowed to man in this adjuftment of things. He can often conceal or difguife his fentiments by the fuppreffion of the natural fign; he can affume appearances, without the feelings to which they belong. In the exercife of this talent he difplays confummate addrefs; and artificial language, more at command, favours the deceit, and countervails the language of nature. Such artifices confer, if I may fay fo, a falfe and temporary phyfiognomy, that violates the connection of things, and belies the fyftem of the mind. So difficult, however, and laborious, is this effort of art, that the moft dexterous diffemblers, aided by all the power of words, often fail in the attempt. A writer, profoundly verfed in the human character, yet more difpofed to heighten

its

its blemishes than its perfections, has remarked, in one of the greatest statesmen of
his time, this struggle between art and nature. "It is, indeed, true," says Dean
Swift of my Lord Somers, " that no man is
" more apt to take fire upon the least ap-
" pearance of provocation, which temper he
" strives to subdue with the utmost violence
" upon himself; so that his breast has been
" seen to heave, and his eyes to sparkle
" with rage, in those very moments when
" his words, and the cadence of his voice,
" were in the humblest and softest manner.
" Perhaps that force upon his nature may
" cause that insatiable love of revenge
" which his detractors lay to his charge,
" who consequently reckon dissimulation
" among his chief perfections *."

To form false combinations is not only
difficult, but the execution probably is al-

* History of the four last Years of the Queen.

ways

ways imperfect; and hence the great masters in expreſſion, whether orators, or actors on the ſtage, muſt endeavour to feel all the emotions they would diſplay to advantage. That becoming attitude, that arrangement of feature they would aſſume, is found attainable only by the medium of correſponding ſentiment. Thus the connection of things is maintained, and we are not deceived, unleſs by attributing a ſolidity and permanency to ſentiments which have ſo unſubſtantial and periſhing an exiſtence. This illuſion of imagination, practiſed on themſelves, and by which alone they compaſs their ends, may even ſway the moral character. In often perſonating the hero, there is acquired a caſt of heroiſm; and in perſonating mean wretches, there is danger of actual debaſement; for ſentiments find an eaſy ingreſs through the imagination into the heart, and the occaſional ſentiments of the actor may become the habitual prin-

ciples

ciples of the man. Thus, the profligate or
libertine, long acted, abates the love of decorum; and he who can suftain the enthufiafm of any virtue, though in a borrowed
character, has probably appropriated to
himfelf fome fhare of its real energy. It is
this mode of proceeding which difcriminates the actor of genius from the inferior
mimic, whofe talents are exhaufted in the
tranfcript of vifible figns, regardlefs of their
foundation in the human mind. In the
one cafe, the reprefentation is juft and natural; in the other, aukward and inani-
mated; and, by fuch criterion, a fagacious
obferver will diftinguifh real excellence
from mechanical imitation in the fictitious
drama, as in the drama of the world, candour from affectation, and the truth of cha--
racter from diffimulation and impofture.

In the interpretation of natural figns,
there is an obvious diftinction to be made
between

between fuch as imply immediate feeling, and the more general, which, without reference to the prefent ftate of the mind, intimate its habitual and predominant temper; as, for inftance, an occafional ftart of good-humour differs from the propenfity which conftitutes a good-humoured man, fo differ their refpective figns. But as frequent returns of the emotion declare the propenfity, fo frequent returns of the correfponding fign tend ultimately to the eftablifhment of a fixed and permanent criterion in the corporeal texture. The particular figns, where no artifice is ufed, are never equivocal; and compofe the firft elements of language. But, as has been before obferved, between the general figns and the temper a repugnancy may often fubfift. In the one cafe, the evidence is explicit; in the other, it is only prefumptive. The former conftitution was expedient or neceffary for the purpofes of focial intercourfe;

courfe; but it was neither neceffary nor expedient, that the character of the mind fhould be legible in the countenance, and in the full view of every beholder.

Upon the whole, it may be concluded, that the mental qualities and the corre-fponding figns are not neceffarily coinci-dent, or the refult of one phyfical arrange-ment, but ftand rather in the relation of caufe and effect; the latter growing out of the former, in confequence of thofe myfte-rious laws which pervade the fyftem of man. Thus moral fentiment diverfifies the outward form; and though the varieties which indicate national character, may of-ten be equally confiftent with health and vigour; yet, in certain circumftances of fociety, there is reafon to believe that the predominant feelings of our nature become highly injurious to the animal œconomy.

5

Let

Let us fuppofe a tribe of mankind reduced to a fituation the moft humiliating and calamitous; cramped in their intellectual exertions by an illiberal difcipline; prone to the fentiments they muft learn to diffemble, and averfe from other fentiments they are obliged to counterfeit; at perpetual variance with fortune; and led, by the rigour of its perfecutions, to cherifh the odious, the rancorous, the vindictive, to the exclufion of all the gentler paffions. Under fuch circumftances, it were contrary to the whole analogy of nature, if the bodily conftitution remained found and untouched. Nor is the picture we have drawn copied from imagination, and affumed merely on the prerogative of hypothefis. The original is, perhaps, to be contemplated in the hiftory of the antient world; among the bondmen of Judea, the helots of Sparta, the fubjects of domeftic tyranny among the Romans. The

C c   condition

condition of thofe tribes was indeed fufficiently wretched : yet fuch as, in fome refpects, might almoft excite envy, when
compared with that feverer deftiny, to
which the maxims of modern policy have
condemned, in another hemifphere, a large
proportion of the fpecies.

Of all the nations of antiquity, the Athenians treated flaves with moft humanity;
the Spartans with the leaft. If, in the treat-
ment of their women, the Spartans have
appeared worthy of fuch fuperior praife;
in this other branch of public manners, they
are far inferior to the rival ftate. The
moft wanton debafement of flaves entered
into the avowed plan of their civil difcipline. The helots were even compelled
to commit vice, in order to infpire an
abhorrence of it in the Spartan youth; to
befot themfelves with intoxicating liquors,
in order to afford a leffon of moderation to

the

the free citizen. But how shocking is that policy which sported with humanity in one form, to give it dignity in another; and authorised a breach of morality, with a view to enforce its precepts ! It is equalled perhaps only by the policy of some modern states, who are said to encourage or connive at the corruption of their priests, with a view to check the influence which superstition is apt to give to that order of men over the minds of the people.

The *Cryptia*, or ambuscade, by which the dark and insidious murder of the helots was authorised by law, casts a dismal shade on the whole fabric of Spartan jurisprudence. It implies a degree of barbarity to which, it must be owned, there is no parallel even in the black code, or in the present regulations of any European state. There is, however, ground to believe that so shocking an institution was suggested on a general revolt of the slaves, by the apprehension of

public

public danger, but difgraced not the fyftem of Lycurgus, nor the purer ages of the Spartan commonwealth. In general, the condition of antient flaves was lefs unhappy. The *Chronia* of the Greeks, the *Saturnalia* of the Romans, could even invert the diftinction of ranks. Slaves, on thefe feftivals, were ferved by their mafters; and all ranks of men were reminded, by an admirable eftablifhment, of that primitive equality which was fuppofed to have fubfifted in the reign of Saturn, and the golden age. Some intervals of freedom were thus permitted; fome fhort refpite to the wretched. But the negro tribes are unacquainted with any fuch indulgences. And, without taxing their American mafters with an inhumanity beyond the nations of antiquity, we may obferve peculiar circumftances in their deftiny that enhance its rigour. Their mafters, without being more inhuman by nature, are, in practice, more unjuft. Antient

tient flaves found a refuge in the fympathy of their mafters, which the negroes do not fo eafily excite. Their features and complexion, regarded as natural badges of inferiority, feem to mark them out for fervitude ; and, furnifhing an occafion for unreafonable contempt, or antipathy approaching to hatred, extinguifh that fellow-feeling with their fufferings, by which their grievances would often be lightened, and the hand of the oppreffor difarmed.

Hatred, envy, and revenge grow up naturally under fuch fufferings. But the love of liberty, the moft ftubborn principle of the heart, is at length eradicated. Self-reverence is gone ; and emancipation itfelf cannot reftore them to the honours of human nature. In time, they view themfelves almoft in the light in which they are viewed by their rulers ; and it is thus they finally acquiefce in their deftiny, and ceafe

C c 3   even

even to think like free men, after having
long ceased to be free.

If then the unfortunate natives of Africa,
the subjects of our dishonourable and odious
commerce, do, in reality, degenerate in the
various regions to which they are transferred,
and, far from multiplying, cannot even keep
up the number of the stock without perpetual recruits, it is not improbable that the
insolence of tyranny, and the violence offered
to the stubborn passions and feelings of nature, contribute as largely to that degeneracy
in their frame, as the smart of the rod, or
malignity of climate, or the labours they
are forced to endure.

The reduction of the negro tribes to
perpetual servitude was contended for in the
fifteenth century, on this notable ground,
" that they had the colour of the damned."
This ground can only be occupied in an
                              ignorant

ignorant and fuperftitious age. But the arguments, by which the fame conduct is ftill attempted to be vindicated, though more fubtle and refined, are equally repugnant to reafon, to humanity, and to found policy. Thofe arguments have accordingly been refuted, from all thefe confiderations, by fome of the moft refpectable writers in our own and other nations; by Hume, by Smith, by Montefquieu; and, in a manner the moft decifive and animated, by an author*, who unites to the warmeft zeal for the rights of mankind, a comprehenfive knowledge of their interefts; and who has adorned a work, abounding in various and ufeful information for all nations, with all the lights of philofophy, and all the fplendor of eloquence. But the conviction of men of fcience is not the conviction of the crowd, and has often but little weight

---

* Hift. Phil. et Polit. tome iv. p. 161 et fuiv.

with

with the rulers of nations; to whom alone it belongs, by prohibiting the importation of flaves under the fevereft penalties, to annihilate for ever a traffic which throws fo great a ftain on the political œconomy of modern ages.

The late refolution of the Quakers in Pennfylvania to emancipate their negro flaves, feems to evidence a degree of pure and difinterefted virtue in that people, beyond the example of the moft virtuous communities of antient times.

The love of civil liberty is furely a generous paffion; yet is it capable of being combined with the love of domination: and it may perhaps be affirmed, that the toleration of domeftic flavery, among the Greeks and Romans, tended to infpire an additional ardour in the caufe of freedom. The feverities inflicted on their flaves

heightened

heightened the dread of their own eventual fufferings. Tyrants at home, they became more jealous of tyranny in their civil rulers, and even impatient under the controul of legal dominion. They contemplated political through the medium of domeftic fervitude, and became in reality more tenacious of civil liberty, by perfifting in a conduct that rendered them more unworthy of it. Perhaps the fame caufe has been productive of fimilar effects in fome of the colonies of America. Yet the nobleft paffion in the human breaft is more naturally cherifhed by the love of juftice and humanity. And it is referved for fome happier age to abolifh, throughout the new hemifphere, an inftitution, which has polluted the hiftory of the freeft governments in the antient world.

In fome of the Spanifh provinces, where the negroes are lefs employed in field-work than

than in domeſtic ſervice, their condition is
ſomewhat elevated; but it is by the depreſ-
ſion of another part of our ſpecies ſtill
more wretched. Submiſſion is more or
leſs humiliating, from the conſideration of
the perſons to whom it is paid. A child is
not degraded by ſubmiſſion to a parent;
nor a ſubject, by allegiance to his lawful
prince. But to be expoſed to the inſults of
a race of ſlaves, is the loweſt form of debaſement. Yet ſuch has been the fortune of
the native Indians in thoſe very countries
where their anceſtors ſuſtained the character
of flouriſhing and happy nations. Among
the inhabitants of the Spaniſh colonies, they
rank below the negroes; who, elevated by
this diſtinction, treat them with inſolence
and ſcorn. And it is the inſidious policy
of the Spaniards, to ſow the ſeeds of diſ-
cord and animoſity between the two races,
who will one day perhaps lay aſide their
mutual rancour, in order to retaliate their

common

common miseries on their imperious masters.

The American features and complexion,
scarce less offensive to the Europeans than
the African, allowed equal scope to their
antipathies; while these antipathies were
heightened and inflamed by the jealousy
entertained of the vanquished. And
though the condition of the Indians is improved by the more recent regulations of
the Spanish policy, had it been possible for
their ancestors at the conquest to have pre-
dicted so long a series of calamity, it might
well have inspired, throughout the empires
of Peru and Mexico, such a desperate reso-
lution, as was actually executed at that æra
by an Indian tribe in the island of Saint
Domingo, who unanimously interdicted
themselves the commerce of sex, that they
might not entail their miseries on a posterity. Thus the Indians in those regions
had

had fuffered extinction, not degradation:
and who would hefitate to prefer the firft,
when fuch alternatives alone are prefented
by fortune ?

But the pen drops from my hand, in
reciting the enormities acted by Europeans in the new hemifphere. Nor
fhould I have entered fo far into the detail,
were I not called upon by my fubject to
contemplate life from its higheft to its
loweft gradation, and to illuftrate thofe
moral fituations, which are fo capable of
producing degeneracy in the human frame.
And fuch confequences may be allowed to
follow from the intimate union of mind
and body, without favouring thofe fyftems
of materialifm, which, however fafhionable
in the philofophy of the prefent age, feem
to confound the moft important diftinctions
of our being. The body, as has been obferved, may profper while the mind is de-
bafed.

bafed. The mind may profper, while the body lofes of its perfection. Yet the fhocks which are felt in the tranfition from a free and happy ftate to that of flavery and dejection, may prove, to the laft degree, injurious to the organization of man. It is not fo much any debafement or elevation of the mental powers, that we have fuppofed deftructive, as unnatural reftraint, as the revolt of the fpirit, and the intenfity of inward emotion. The limit of this influence over a people, we pretend not to fix with precifion; yet that the contagion of the mind, in a variety of ways, affects the whole animal œconomy, is eftablifhed by the hiftory of individuals, of tribes, and of nations. And as the condition of a flave is by far the moft wretched in the lot of man, fo its tendency is apparently the moft deftructive. Of this, the hiftory of the negro tribes furnifhes an immenfe variety of the moft melancholy

melancholy examples. And it is fufficiently attefted, that great numbers of
the native Indians of America, when they
found they were treated as flaves by the
Spaniards, have died of vexation, or deftroyed themfelves in the frenzy of defpair. Under the rigour then of fuch
difcipline, we may expect the decline of
the animal fyftem, if not the total extinction of the degraded race.

But the perfection of the animal is
not the perfection of the man; neither
do their infirmities neceffarily correfpond.
It is therefore of more importance to
enquire how far moral and civil culture
affects the fyftem of the mind, and thereby creates original and effential differences
in the temper and genius of pofterity: a
queftion which, promifing fome farther
openings into the theory of the human
character, deferves to be confidered in
a feparate Effay.

ESSAY XIII.

OF THE HEREDITARY GENIUS OF NATIONS.

THE empire of the imagination and the paffions, .by diverfifying the natural form, and reaching the organization of man, has appeared to be extenfive. But, without invigorating or enervating the principle of mere animal life, perhaps his genius and character in one age may, by the more direct laws of the intellectual œconomy, affect the original genius and character of fucceeding generations. The mode of this œconomy we pretend not to unfold. It is the order of things ; it is the relation of appearances alone, which is the foundation of all juft theory with regard to

the

the natural or to the moral world. The connection of cause and effect is, in all cases, a
mysterious connection, which no mortal
can unveil. Prior then to all theory, let us
contemplate some of the appearances in
civil life.

The separation of families and the
distinction of ranks are essential to all
political establishments. No division of
property, no rules of patrimonial succession,
no sumptuary, no agrarian laws can long
preserve a parity of rank or fortune among
any people. The greater number, indeed,
in every state, are rendered subservient to
the few; are confounded together in one
class, and compose the rude vulgar of mankind. Thus, in the plan of the Comitia
of Rome, the people was distributed into
six classes, and every Roman was allowed
some share of political power; but the
lowest class gradually sunk into neglect.

The

The whole power of the comitia was transferred to their fuperiors, and thofe of each clafs, though equal in their collective capacity, were, as men and as citizens, of very unequal confideration.

Thefeus inftituted at Athens an order of nobility, and debarred the people at large from all the honourable functions of civil government. And if Solon, by permitting every citizen to vote in the public affembly, feemed to confer on the meaneft of them a fort of political exiftence; yet, even by Solon's plan, the Athenians were divided into three claffes, according to the extent of their fortunes, while the mafs of the people, diftinct from thefe, were legally excluded from all offices of truft or honour.

In Sparta alone an equality of fortune was the aim of the legiflator, and an avowed maxim of government. But the expedients

D d

of

of Lycurgus were not effectual for that
purpose ; and, even in the pureft ages of
the Commonwealth, the diftinction of riches
and poverty was not totally unknown.

Such is the condition of men in the moft
democratical ftates. The forms of fociety
require fubordination ; the detail of affairs
calls for different occupations ; and mankind
are diftributed into claffes, to which belong
unequal degrees of importance.

That the fubdivifion of arts, which is fo
conducive to their perfection, degrades the
character of the common artizan, is a propofition confonant to the uniform experience of civilized nations. The moft fimple manufacture is executed by the joint
labour of a number of people, each of
whom being expert only in his own peculiar branch, perceives neither the connection of defign, nor the refult of the combination.

bination. That fyftematic knowledge belongs only to the mafter-artift ; and the detail of the execution feems to refemble, in fome fort, the proceedings of inftinct in animal life, where we fo often obferve, by the wifdom of nature, a regular, though blind, co-operation of numbers towards an unknown end.

The manufacture of a pin is a trite example, ferving well to illuftrate this fubdivifion of labour. That bufinefs is fubdivided into about eighteen diftinct operations, which are fometimes all performed by diftinct hands. In manufactures of a more complicated fabric, the operations are ftill farther fubdivided, and often tend, among the various orders of artizans, to debilitate the body, and to engender difeafe. But exclufively of this confequence, the life of fuch an artizan is filled up with a feries of actions, which, returning with an infipid

uniform-

uniformity, affords no exercife to genius or capacity. And if the tendency of his occupation is not counteracted by fome expedient of government, he is fuffered to fall into a torpor of intellect, which implies the abfence or annihilation of every manly virtue. Such occupations, in the antient republics of Greece and Rome, were confidered as beneath the dignity of free citizens, and were commonly exercifed by flaves.

In the prefent ftate of the arts among the European nations, perhaps the moft refpectable character among the inferior ranks is bred by the profeffion of arms. Its functions, which have more compafs and variety, are more animated and interefting than thofe of a mechanical trade. The whole detail of military exercife polifhes and fafhions the body, and even confers graces which elevate the mind. In the

breaft

breaſt of a private ſoldier, accordingly, there often reigns a ſenſe of perſonal dignity and honour, which ſcarce ever enters into the maſs of the people, and is but rarely to be met with in men of ſuperior affluence and figure. A certain caſt of genius and character adheres to every condi- tion. Different degrees of refinement and civility characteriſe the various orders of citi- zens; and the dignity or meanneſs annexed to the ſphere in which they move, is, by no violent tranſition of imagination, trans- ferred to their immediate, and even to re- mote deſcendents, and regarded as appen- dages of poſterity.

Thus families are formed, where men become deſtined, from birth alone, to oc- cupy, in civil ſociety, more or leſs exalted ſtations. Antiquity of family then implies a deſcent from a ſeries of anceſtors long ſe- parated from the crowd, and exalted to ſome eminence in the ranks of life. Now,

D d 3 it

it will not be denied, that in the firſt generation, the reſemblance of children to parents is often conſpicuous in the features,
both of body and mind. The one ſpecies of
reſemblance is ſometimes conſpicuous where
the other is ſcarce diſcernible; and the
other ſpecies is ſometimes no leſs predómi-
nant where the former ſubſiſts in an inferior, or perhaps in no degree. Theſe principles, though blended occaſionally in their
operations, ſeem to be diſtinct and inde-
-pendent. Various cauſes, to us unknown,
may interrupt the law of reſemblance in
the outward form. Various cauſes, alike
unknown, may interrupt the law of reſemblance in the moral œconomy. Theſe
connections and dependencies we attempt
not to explore. We know not how far the
character of parents touches, if we may ſay
ſo, the elements of the amorous paſſion, or
diverſifies the mode of inſtinct, ſo as to
affect the progeny of phyſical love. It is
ſufficient, if general experience declare ſuch
connections

connections to have a foundation in nature.

Admit then, that certain qualities of mind, as well as body, are tranfmiffible in the firft generation, and do not terminate there ; is there not reafon to expect, from the accumulated efforts of the fame caufes, that fome general inheritance may be derived in a courfe of ages, and confequently, that a greater or lefs propenfity to refinement, to civility, and to the politer arts, may be connected with an illuftrious, or more obfcure original ?

But this fpecies of influence, which is ftrictly moral, ought to be variable in every country, with the order, the policy, and the arrangements of civil fociety. It is the genius of popular and free governments to annihilate, in fome fort, family diftinctions. Citizens, born to equal privileges, and con-

ftituted

ftituted in fimilar points of exterior rank,
will tranfmit to pofterity more equal proportions of the gifts of nature. Under a
more unequal government, where diftinctions abound, where there reigns the
ftrongeft contraft of circumftances, and
where a difparity of condition has been
cherifhed and preferved for ages, the moral
diverfity will be more confpicuous; and
civil diftinctions long maintained, will open
a fource of natural diftinctions in fucceeding times. Hereditary characteriftics accordingly attracted the attention of mankind, in fome degree, under all the antient
governments. A regard to defcent, which
amounted to a fpecies of idolatry among
fome nations, has not been altogether exploded in free and popular ftates. In the
Gentoo government of Indoftan, the diftinction of cafts or tribes was never violated
by promifcuous commerce. And fuch was
the public folicitude of the Indians, about
the

the future generation, that phyſical education might be ſaid to commence antecedently
to birth. A guardian was appointed for an
infant yet unborn; and it was his province
to lay down a regimen for the mother
during the months of pregnancy *.

The improvement of the race of citizens
was a favourite objeat of Spartan policy.
And while, with this view, the laws authoriſed, under certain regulations, a community of wives, and even approved of croſſ-
ing the brood, they permitted not alliances
or intermarriages among the different orders of citizens. Such alliances and intermarriages were alſo expreſsly interdiated
by the laws of Rome, for upwards of three
hundred years. The free ſpirit of the Romans indeed at laſt rebelled againſt ſuch
odious diſtinaions, and opened to every
citizen the way to civil honours. Yet the

* Gentoo Code, p. 283.

Romans

Romans themfelves, after fo glorious a
ftruggle for privilege, againft the ufurpations of a proud nobility, teftified, in the
very moment of victory, their reverence
for Patrician blood*. Imagination furely,
in all fuch cafes, influences the judgment
of the people; and while it inclines them
fo often to beftow unmerited preference, it
fometimes elevates the character of the individuals to whom that preference is given.
Men nobly born are animated with the idea,
and think themfelves called upon, in a peculiar manner, to emulate the virtues, and
to fuftain the honours of their name.

Et Pater Anchifes, & avunculus excitat Hector.

They feel, not what they are, but what
they ought to be; till at laft, by feeling
what they ought to be, they become what
they were not: and thus by reverencing

* Tit. Liv. cap. 6, lib. iv.

the

the dignity of anceftors, they learn to aflert
their own. But, independently of fuch
fentiments, as well as of all the peculiar
incentives to true glory, there is often an
invifible preparation of natural caufes,
which concurs with the civil order of
things in prolonging the honours or even
the infamy of a race ; and hereditary
characteriftics are interwoven into the genius and effence of the mind. Hence the
milder glories of the *Valerii*; hence the unfeeling obftinacy and infolence of the *Ap-*
pian blood. And, perhaps, it will be found
that the judgment of the crowd, in thefe, as
in many inftances, though fwayed by imagination, has however a foundation in experience, and is, in part, conformable to
general laws,

To vindicate the principle on which
this judgment proceeds, let us review
the condition of a family emerging
from rudenefs into the dignity of civil
life.

life. Let us fuppofe the founders conftituted in a ftate of independence, and of
decent affluence; graced with every circumftance that can command refpect; improved by all the advantages of moral and
of civil culture, and exalted to a mode of
thinking, and of acting, fuperior to vulgar
minds. Some traces of this fpirit, we may
affirm, without being charged with exceffive
refinement, are likely to adhere to their
immediate progeny. But, how fcanty or
latent foever this inheritance at firft, if the
caufes are not difcontinued, the conftitutional effect will be more confpicuous in
the fecond generation. If the former
impreffions are not effaced, the third
generation will have their conftitution
more ftrongly impregnated with the fame
elements; till at laft, by happy alliances,
and by preferving the line on one fide
long unbroken, there fhall refult an affociation of qualities, which, being con-
folidated into the conftitution, form the

charac-

characteriftics of a race. The fame reafoning is eafily transferred to a family of an
ignoble line. Inftead of competence, independence, culture, fubftitute indigence, fer-
vility, rudencfs. Extend this allotment
over an equal feries of pofterity, and you
will probably reverfe all the propenfities of
nature. A thoufand circumftances indeed
may warp a conftitution from any line of
character, and be deftructive of all hereditary fymptoms; but if thefe fymptoms
are often found to be concomitants of birth,
and are vifible in the extremes, they will
fubfift, though lefs apparently, in other fituations; and our reafoning, how fallacious foever, if applied to individuals,
juftifies the general conclufion. If that
turn of imagination, thofe infirmities of
intellect, which mark infanity, or delirium,
or folly, are fo often confeffed hereditary,
fhall we not allow to all the noble endowments and talents of the mind, the fame
prero-

prerogative ? But there is no need to infer from analogy what might be eſtabliſhed by the moſt copious induction, were it not tedious to enumerate particulars, where the experience of common life is ſo deciſive. Theſe communicable qualities are ſubject to many contingencies : ſome are obliterated ; others, checked in their growth, lie dormant for generations, yet again revive : it is only an aſſemblage of great talents, or the long predominance of ſome one ſtriking quality, that attracts the obſervation of the world. The great qualities of the laſt Athenian king flouriſhed in the *Archons* for above three hundred years. The *Incas* of Peru, during a far longer period, were eminent for every princely virtue. The daughter of *Scipio* was mother of the *Gracchi.* The heroiſm of the younger *Brutus* was the heroiſm of his remote progenitor. The houſes of the *Publicolæ,* the *Meſſalæ,*

5 and

and *Valerii*, were illuſtrious for ſix hundred years. The *Decii*, retaining, equally long, their primeval character, attempted the re-vival of Roman virtue in the decline of the empire. And, if expectation might be raiſed upon ſuch foundations, a Briton might almoſt anticipate ſome of the actors on the public ſtage at ſome future æra. We have ſeen a patron of freedom in our days, infe-rior to no Roman name, commanding the applauſe of ſenates, ſuſtaining the vigour of public councils, and leading on a nation to glory. We have ſeen another, of conge-nial ſpirit, preſiding in the aſſembly of the nobles, and diſpenſing, from the higheſt tribunal, juſtice to the people ;

―― His dantem Jura Catonem.

I dare not mention a name among the living―but that the moſt illuſtrious ſtateſ-man of the preſent age has left poſterity, is matter of generous ſatisfaction to the Engliſh nation.

Yet

Yet we are far from confidering birth as the criterion of any one perfection of the mind or body. Neither do we fuppofe, in general, that an exalted ftation calls forth the greateft talents, or is moft favourable to the growth, or communication of moral or intellectual endowments. Thofe in the middle ranks of life, in a flourifhing and cultivated nation, promife to tranfmit as fair an inheritance to pofterity. The accefs to refinement, to culture, and to civil honours, which is opened to them in the progrefs of government, allows them almoft every advantage ; while they are often exempted from corruptions which are foftered by fuperior rank. Without drawing invidious parallels, it may be affirmed, that the fluctuation of things, in our age and country, the rotation of employments, the mutual intercourfes, intermarriages, and alliances, fo often formed, are fufficient to blend and unite different

tempers

tempers and capacities, fo as to prevent hereditary endowments from becoming cha-racteriſtical of any one order of citizens: Yet the fame caufes, whofe influence in particular families is ſtill fufficient to draw attention, might, in other circumſtances of fociety, have affected the departments of civil life, and the more general diviſions of mankind. In ancient times, when pro-feſſions were hereditary; when inter-marriages among different claſſes were not permitted, or were held diſhonour-able; when conjugal love was rarely vio-lated, and genealogy was a faſhionable fcience; hereditary talents would be more obfervable, and their influence in fociety more ſtrongly defined. Upon the whole, it muſt be admitted, that the character of anceſtors has influence on the line of poſterity; and that a long feries of caufes, antecedent to birth, has affected, in each individual, not only the mechanical and

E e

vital

vital fprings, but, in fome degree alfo, the
conftitutional arrangements of his intellectual nature. The circumftance therefore of birth alone, may be regarded as
more or lefs aufpicious; and may be
allowed, on fome occafions, to heighten or
to deprefs expectation; but cannot, without
palpable and egregious abfurdity, enter
farther into the account, or be rendered a
topic of exultation or reproach in the eftimation of perfonal merit. Iphicrates, an
upftart Athenian, replied with becoming
fpirit to a perfon of noble birth, who had
dared to arraign his pedigree, " The ho-
" nours of my family begin with myfelf:
" the honours of yours end in you." How
often might thofe in a humble fphere, exchange places with men who fit in the
cabinet of kings? how often, as in the
Roman government, might we call a Dictator from the plough? The diftinction
here opened, far from flattering the arro-

6   gance,

gance, or juftifying the ufurpations of men,
if extended from individuals, and families,
to the larger affociations of mankind, will
help to explain the hiftory of the world
with the leaft poffible violence to the common prerogatives of the fpecies.

A cultivated and polifhed nation may, in
fome refpects, be regarded as a ftanding
family. The one is, relatively to the
greater number of the communities of
mankind, what the other is, relatively to
the greater number of citizens under the
fame civil œconomy. The conduct of the
one, and of the other, towards their fuppofed inferiors, is often exactly fimilar.
Both carry themfelves with equal infolence,
and feem alike to forget or to deny the
inherent and unalienable rights of the
fpecies. Nations, however, as well as
families, may have fome inheritance to
boaft; and the progeny of favages or bar-

E e 2

barians may be diftinguifhable, both in outward and inward form, from the progeny of a cultivated people. A long feries of civilization may exalt and refine certain 'principles congenial to our frame. A long feries of ages fpent in rudenefs or barbarity, may blunt and disfigure, though it can never obliterate, in any tribe, the great outlines of human nature. While one feries of caufes tends more effectually to the perfection of the animal powers, another feries may prove more aufpicious to fome parts of the intellectual œconomy. Many favage tribes are remarkable for abilities in one line, while no lefs deficient in another. Some difcover fingular, and almoft incredible propenfities to manners approaching to brutality. The indocility of others is perfectly aftonifhing. And in general, as if reluctant to diveft themfelves of the habits of their anceftors, they fhew an unfitnefs to receive the graces and refinements of polifhed life.

life. Such appearances are afcribed by fome writers to a fixed and immutable diverfity in the races of mankind ; and the regions that by accident have been the fcene of rudenefs and barbarity, are pointed out as the permanent and natural habitations of inferior mortals. But thefe innate and conftitutional differences have been fhewn, in the preceding pages, to be fluctuating and contingent ; and therefore confiftent with parity of rank, and one common origin of nations.

Allow to the moft unpromifing tribes fuch advantages in the political fcene, as belong occafionally to the rudeft vulgar, under any civil eftablifhment ; and as the latter emerge into dignity among their fellow-citizens, fo fhall the former among the fociety of nations. The inheritances of all the families within a ftate, reckoning from its firft foundation, are, perhaps, nearly ba-

lanced

lanced in the revolution of the great year of government. The inheritances of tribes and nations in all countries of the globe, may be also balanced in the revolution of that greater year which completes the deſtiny of man.

Illuſtrious rank is no more to be regarded as a criterion of perfection in forming the general eſtimate of nations, than in forming the particular eſtimate of the ſeveral families or members of the ſame community. The greateſt nation is not always bleſſed with the moſt equal government, nor adorned with the moſt accompliſhed citizens. The collective wiſdom of a people is not to be eſtimated by that proportion of it which actuates their public councils, or even by the detail of their civil government. Yet that government is certainly, in one reſpect, well conſtituted, that calls abilities and diſtinguiſhed worth into public view.   Sir
William

William Temple has pronounced this eu-
logium on the conftitution of the United
Provinces of Holland, though rather at
the expence of the national character.
"Though perhaps the nation, fays that
" writer, generally be not wife, yet the go-
" vernment is, becaufe it is compofed of the
" wifeft of the nation, which may give it
" an advantage over many others, where
" ability is of more common growth, but
" of lefs ufe to the public, if it happens
" that neither wifdom nor honefty are the
" qualities which bring men to the manage-
" ment of ftate affairs, as they ufually do
" in this commonwealth." It is, however,
no fmall point of wifdom to diftinguifh fuperior worth ; and the men who are difpofed
to regard with juft admiration noble talents, are inferior only to the men who
poffefs them.

But it may be queftioned, whether the
happieft periods, even of free governments,

are the periods moſt conducive to the perfections of mankind. Perhaps the higheſt
national, as well as private virtue, is bred
in the ſchool of adverſity. A nation certainly may derive ſplendour from thoſe
very circumſtances which ſink the character of its citizens. The ſcience of me-
chanics, which is the glory of human reaſon, has enlarged the abilities, and dignified
the aſpect of nations. Yet the lower claſſes
of artizans and manufacturers, in moſt of
the civilized governments of modern Europe, who are ſo inſtrumental in promoting
public opulence and commercial proſperity,
may be pronounced to be themſelves in a
ſtate of intellectual debaſement, to which
there is ſcarce any parallel in the hiſtory of
rude barbarians. It is active and progreſſive
virtue; it is refinement of manners, or vigour of ſentiment, and the habits of intellectual exertion, which confer real honour
on families; it is the more general and dif-
fuſive influence of ſimilar habits, that ex-
alts

alts a people in a moral light, and enriches their genius for generations to come.

But the genius of man is fo flexible, fo open to impreffions from without, fo fufceptible of early culture, that between hereditary, innate, and acquired propenfities, it is hard to draw the line of diftinction. It were neceffary that the natives of one country fhould be bred up and educated, from their earlieft infancy, among the natives of another, in order to make fair experiments with regard to original talents. Under fuch circumftances, individuals are occafionally prefented to view. A Theban may be bred at Athens, an Athenian in Bœotia. And, if whole tribes of mankind could be placed in fimilar fituations, we might then indeed contemplate them in their innate, as well as in their acquired characteriftics, obferve the one mingling with, or checked by the other, and mark,

in

in a variety of combinations, their accumulated influence. Qualities, however,
that refift for ages the change of government and of climate, muft be allowed to be
congenial and hereditary to the tribes
among whom they are found to predominate.

Perhaps the hiftory of the Jews furnifhes an example of a race, whofe peculiar
qualities, thus circumftanced, have defcended through a long courfe of generations. No people, it may be affirmed,
have ever figured on the theatre of nations,
with a deftiny as fingular as theirs. Their
hiftory, whether drawn from facred or profane records, whether regarded as miracu-
lous, or in the order of nature, affords
matter of abundant fpeculation. The
maxims of their religion and policy preferved them in all the revolutions of fortune, as a diftinct people. After the final
diffolution

diffolution of their government, and difperfion all over the habitable globe, a fyftem of prejudices peculiar to themfelves,
but directed, in its operations, to fulfil the
ends of Providence, has preferved their genealogy, and prevented alliances or intermarriages with any other race. Certain
marks of uniformity are accordingly difcernible among them in every period.
The fame fpirit which was fo untractable
under their own governors, difpofed them
to mutiny and rebellion when a Roman
province; and that perverfenefs of temper,
which led them fo often to apoftacy and to
idolatry, when in poffeffion of the true
faith, has rendered them tenacious of a falfe
religion. As numerous, perhaps, at this
day, as when a fettled nation, the relation
of confanguinity, under all the various governments and climates where their lot is
caft, marks their character. Yet, had this
infociable people remained in their antient
poffeffions,

possessions, and, without foreign connections
or intermarriages, had subsisted under the
same political establishment, the most singular, surely, that ever was formed, the
lineaments of their character, both of inward and outward form, had, we may well
believe, been still more strongly defined.
In general it may be observed, that the
confined intercourse of the species tends
ultimately to the formation of a peculiar
genius and temper. Thus, in the antient
Germans, the uniformity of individuals
was as astonishing as the diversity of all
from every other people; and, from the
singularity of these appearances, the Roman
historian supposes them a pure and distinct
race, not derived from Asia, from Africa,
from Italy, or from any other region *.

The new hemisphere presented appearances exactly similar. The astonishing re-

* Tacit. de Mor. Germ.

semblance

femblance which was there obferved among mankind, feems to evidence that it was peopled originally by the fame race, and at an æra of no high antiquity. The branches, though widely fpread, had probably not been long feparated from the common ftock; or perhaps a fimilarity in the modes of life contributed, more than any other caufe, throughout that immenfe continent, to exclude variety in the human fpecies.

The hiftory of Indoftan, where the *Aborigines* are fo clearly defined from the other natives of the fame regions, might be mentioned as another ftriking example of a genius and conftitution which confanguinity has in part contributed to cherifh and preferve for ages.

When emigrants from different countries, fixed in one fettlement, and under one political œconomy, preferve, however, for a
length

length of time, diftinguifhing characteriftics, the diverfity cannot be altogether afcribed to circumftances pofterior to birth. The temper of the Britifh nation, which is attributed by fome writers to local fituation, flourifhes with equal vigour in another hemifphere. The fpirit which now animates American councils, was the fpirit of Britons in a former age; and the Britons, in the fame province, are diftinguifhable from every other tribe. The concourfe of fo many tribes proved, in the Britifh colonies, a fertile fource of animofity and diffenfion; and unfortunate, furely, was that policy in the parent ftate, which could fo far fubdue the antipathies, and reconcile the prejudices of fo mixed a people, as to unite them in one general confederacy againft her government. Yet perhaps this temporary and precarious union may diffolve apace; the feeds of internal difcord may revive; and their mutual jealoufies, if not con-
trouled

trouled by superior wisdom, may one day shake the foundations of this rising empire, or reunite it to the British government.

But were all memorials of these settlements rescinded from modern annals, there might be observed for ages to come, constitutional distinctions in the same province, where the greater number, from constitutional resemblances, might boast of one lineage with Britons. Yet, these resemblances, and those distinctions, time must annihilate. And, from a new order of things, there must finally arise that peculiar association of qualities, which is properly called national, as distinguishing a people long under the same physical and moral œconomy, from the rest of the world.

Much latitude, however, is allowed in the genius and character of every people, without violation of the general law. What

variety

variety among children of the fame parents,
do we obferve to confift with a family refemblance? Confiftent, in the fame manner,
with family characteriftics, is a certain
national uniformity; and confiftent with
national characteriftics, are the effentials of
a common nature, and a common defcent.
Such varieties ought not to create antipathies, or unhinge, or even relax the focial
ties. On the contrary, if it hold in man,
that croffing the brood tends occafionally
to improvement, this confideration, which
forms a natural argument againft inceft, fo
juftly prohibited on political and moral
grounds by all civilized and enlightened
governments, authorifes and invites all
nations to form mutual connexions and
alliances.

Thus we may obferve mankind, effen-
tially the fame, yet in different regions of
the globe, varying continually from a fixed
ftandard;

ſtandard; breathing at firſt, if I may uſe the expreſſion, unequal proportions of the ætherial ſpirit; excelling in the rational, in the moral, or in the animal powers; born with a ſuperior fitneſs for refinement, for arts, for civil culture; or caſt in a rougher mould, and by native temper more indocible and wild. Yet all the capital diſtinctions in individuals, families or tribes, flow from cauſes ſubſequent to birth; from education, example, forms of government; from the order of internal laws, from the maxims and genius of religion, from the lights of ſcience and philoſophy; in ſome degree from the infallible operations of the external elements; but above all, from the free determinations of the will. To run the parallel of nations, and decide on their comparative perfections, were a deſign too aſpiring for the Author of theſe Eſſays; yet the appearances in civil life we may pronounce to be often deluſive. The

F f   manners,

manners, the crimes of illiterate favage tribes are apt enough to appear to us in their full dimenfion and deformity; but the violations of natural law among civilized nations have a folemn varnifh of policy, which difguifes the enormity of guilt. The greatnefs too of a community dazzles the eye, and confers an imaginary value on its members. It eclipfes the milder luftre of more humble tribes. Yet the virtue of nations, as of individuals, frequently courts the fhade, and the beautiful figure of the poet is equally applicable to both :

Full many a flower is born to blufh unfeen,
And wafte its fweetnefs on the defert air.

Hiftory, which ought to be the miftrefs of human life, affects magnificence, and feems to defcend from her dignity in recording the tranfactions of little States. She forgets that men may grow lefs by elevation, and
permits

permits the honours of nations to be diftributed by the hands of fortune. It is hence
the Greeks and Romans are regarded by
us, with a veneration fo far above all the
nations of antiquity. Hence Europe, in
modern times, boafts a pre-eminence that
feems to infult the reft of the world.

It belongs to reafon and philofophy to
re-judge mankind; and, under an endlefs
variety of appearances, more or lefs equivocal, to obferve and fix the principles
which affeæt, in every age and country,
the proportion of human happinefs, and of
human perfeætion. Let not nations then,
or individuals, regard themfelves as fingle
in the creation; let them view their interefts on the largeft fcale; let them feel
the importance of their ftation to themfelves and to the fyftem; to their contemporaries, and to future generations; and
learn, from the eftablifhed order of fecond
caufes,

caufes, to refpect, to adorn, and to exalt the fpecies.

Nor is the detail of the meaneft tribes unimportant in philofophy. If human nature is liable to degenerate, it is capable of proportionable improvement from the collected wifdom of ages. It is pleafant to infer, from the actual progrefs of fociety, the glorious poffibilities of human excellence. And, if the principles can be affembled into view, which moft directly tend to diverfify the genius and character of nations, fome theory may be raifed on thefe foundations, that fhall account more fyftematically for paft occurrences, and afford fome openings and anticipations into the eventual hiftory of the world.

THE END.

www.ingramcontent.com/pod-product-compliance
Lightning Source LLC
Chambersburg PA
CBHW031101110726
47900CB00003B/1010